SPEAKING GLOBALLY

SPEAKING GLOBALLY

Effective Presentations
Across International
and Cultural
Boundaries

Elizabeth Urech

Completely Revised and Updated
Second Edition

SMITH/KERR ASSOCIATES LLC

Inquiries concerning reproduction outside those terms should be sent to the publishers at the undermentioned address:
Smith/Kerr Associates LLC
207.439.2921
Bizbks@aol.com
www.SmithKerr.com

ISBN: 0-9717615-1-5

Illustrations by Thomas Urech
Cover design by Claire MacMaster

For information about Speaking Unlimited programs and keynote speeches, please contact:
Speaking Unlimited
312.913.9071
beth@speakingunlimited.com
www.speakingunlimited.com

Printed in the United States of America.

Table of Contents

Introduction

For commerce and industry, our global village is becoming a reality, but political events threaten to splinter our world into fragments. Concurrently, as electronic communication gets faster and easier, misunderstandings are proliferating. That is why it is increasingly important to be cognizant of other cultures and informed about people who see the world from a different perspective.

Speaking Globally will benefit you in any public speaking situation and is of prime interest when you are speaking internationally. You need not travel to a foreign country to find my book a valuable resource. Refer to it before you speak at an international conference in your home country and whenever you communicate in a multi-lingual and culturally-diverse environment.

Speaking Globally offers easy-to-learn techniques which you can put into practice quickly. You will learn how to:

- control your nerves
- use your hands effectively
- stand and move with purpose
- engage your audience's WIIFM ("What's in it for me?")
- create a powerful PowerPoint slide show
- deal with hecklers and confrontational journalists
- give your listeners a take-home message to really take home.

Once you know how to create and deliver a winning message, you are ready to tackle the global arena. In the Country Profiles you will learn how to tailor your message for specific audiences, including whether or not it is appropriate to

❂ use first names when you meet

❂ greet VIPs before you begin speaking

❂ shake hands

❂ make direct eye contact

❂ toast by clinking glasses

Some readers may wonder why such customs really matter. Quite simply, your behavior influences how you, your firm and your home country are perceived. For example, beginning to speak without properly acknowledging the VIPs in your audience may be insulting to your hosts. In some countries, not making eye contact when offering a toast is considered rude. In some cultures crossing your legs when seated and showing the soles of your shoes could be a deal-breaker. You want be able to navigate between cultures and build bridges for successful relationships worldwide.

Of course, as you strive to avoid pitfalls and *faux pas*, you need to maintain your individuality. In every business presentation there is room for warmth and humor, particularly to break the ice and untie the knot of political correctness. Don't aim for perfection; aim to make a connection.

Speaking Globally is based upon my work with hundreds of clients from every continent. Some of them are the CEOs of major multinationals; others are just starting up the ladder of success. No matter how much they may have doubted their speaking ability at the outset, all of them have learned how to face an audience with confidence, authority and ease.

If you are reading these words on the way to a conference where you will be speaking, please turn to "Last Minute Changes." Until you put your foot on the platform, you still have time to improve.

Now, accept the challenge! With *Speaking Globally* in hand, you will find unlimited opportunities to speak for yourself!

CHAPTER 1

Determine Your Desired End Results

"My big weakness is preparation. I'm not good at it. I admit it. I procrastinate," admitted the CEO of an international biotechnology firm. "What is more important to me is the business of the day. I know that is wrong because the day before or when I'm standing on the podium, I think, 'I should have made this speech a priority.'"

Sound familiar? No matter how far in advance you agree to give a speech, eventually the day will dawn when you are headed for the lectern. Unless you enjoy writing speeches, you are probably guilty of procrastinating.

You need not prepare your entire speech months in advance, but you really ought to ask yourself three questions: When you finish speaking, how do you want your audience to react? How do you want to come across? What one specific fact or message do you want your audience to remember two weeks later?

When I work with a client, we spend an average of one hour discussing these questions and formulating the answers. Sounds like a lot of time, doesn't it? But if you do this preparatory work, you will reap dividends as the weeks fly by and you consider what to include in your speech and how to make it memorable for your audience. You can try it for yourself by completing the statements in Figure 1.1 on p. 2. Let's go through these three points step by step.

FIGURE 1.1 Three statements on your desired end result

DESIRE
(Desired End Results)

1. When I finish my presentation, I want my audience to _____

_____

(Complete the sentence using an active verb, such as fly, buy, try.)

2. I want to come across as

_____

_____

_____

(Choose three descriptive terms, such as thorough, dynamic, buoyant.)

3. Two weeks later, I want my audience to remember

_____

(Choose one very specific word or fact, such as: "Networking" or "The cost was zero.")

What Do You Want Your Audience to Do When You Finish Speaking?

If your first reaction is to say, "Applaud," that's wonderful. That is how an audience says "thank you" for the effort you have spent preparing and practicing. Then what would you like your audience to do? If you choose a verb like "appreciate" or "understand," you are off to a weak start. To be candid, an audience can "understand or appreciate" your company's goals for global expansion and still doze off. It often happens.

Determine the strongest appeal you can make to an audience. The stronger it is, the more urgency and energy you will bring to your speech and the better reaction you will get in return. If at all possible, get them actively involved. Ask them to do something:

❂ When I finish my talk, I want you to fly my airline.

❂ When I finish my talk, I want you to buy these mutual funds.

❂ When I finish my talk, I want you to try our new polymers.

When you speak, strive to build a dynamic tension with your audience. Recently, I asked a client how he wanted his audience to react. He answered, "I want them to see that the Czech Republic has great potential." In actual fact, he was speaking at an investment summit, and he wanted to convince the audience to pump money into his country. Once he started trying to actively involve his audience, his talk became dynamic and stimulating. In his presentation, he never actually said the words, "invest in my country, dammit," but it was the underlying message.

How Do You Want to Come Across?

When you stand up to speak, an audience looks you over, listens to you and makes an appraisal. It may be incomplete and inaccurate, but it is often lasting. Since people do label speakers, why not get ahead of the game by determining how you want to come across before you are headed for the lectern. By the way, the lectern is what you stand behind; the podium is the raised platform you stand upon.

The overwhelming majority of my clients plead, "I just want to be myself!" Which is great. An audience also wants to see the "real you." Unfortunately most speakers change remarkably in front of an audience and not for the better. They don a bland business mask, minimize gestures and speak in a flat unemotional voice.

The more you risk showing who you really are, the better your presentation will be. Of course, thirty minutes is not long enough to let your audience appreciate everything that makes you unique. You have to choose which facets of your personality to display. And your choice will be different for every presentation.

A Swedish engineer was giving a "make or break" presentation to his head office in San Diego. He needed to prove that he was not only a manager but that he could operate in a sales and marketing role. He wanted to come across as "thorough, dynamic and buoyant." In this context, "thorough" is an obvious choice, especially for an engineer. Wanting to appear "dynamic" in a speech to senior management also makes good sense. The word "buoyant" is perhaps an odd choice, but this speaker's goal was to show top management that he had the buoyancy — unusual in an engineer — to excel at marketing and sales. He gave a buoyant presentation and was later promoted.

You may not choose the word "buoyant," but do find an image which enables you to stay afloat!

What Do You Want Your Audience to Remember Two Weeks after You Speak?

Audiences have poor attention spans and terrible memories. Studies show that audiences forget 50 percent of what you say within 24 hours. They forget 90 percent of what you say within two weeks.

What one fact or word do you want your audience to remember for two weeks? It might be the name of your company or your desired end result. Phrase it as the very last sentence of your presentation. Then memorize it. That is where you are headed. In order for your audience to remember your message, they need to see it, hear it, taste it, smell it. You need to paint a picture of it.

As the final sentence of his presentation for Dow's First Paint Seminar, Piotr Drezewicz chose the sentence: "We're painting Poland in the picture."

"We're painting Poland in the picture" is an idiom that worked well for three reasons. First, the product was paint. Second, Poland is a grayish country which is moving forward and is more "in the picture" in the world's eye. And third, the audience was Polish. They liked that message!

Can you write your take-home message in one sentence? If you can't, it probably isn't ready yet.

In a talk about *The Power of Positioning*, Sue Coupland of Rothwell & Coupland, The Positioning Company, stressed, "You have to be able to telephone your mother and state your concept in one sentence that she can understand. If you can't, then your idea isn't clear or focused enough." Spontaneously, Sue walked over to the first row of delegates' tables, reached into a plate of jelly beans and tossed a single jelly bean to an amazed delegate who caught it. She threw a second jelly bean to another delegate who caught it. Finally, Sue threw a handful of jelly beans to a third delegate who couldn't catch any of them. She concluded: "It is the same thing with ideas. Choose a single message and focus it, so your customer can catch it."

To make sure that your take-home message gets taken home, you need to hone it until it is simple and clear. Your words need to be strong and resounding. And they need to be exactly right for your audience.

Determine Your Audience's WIIFM

WIIFM is an acronym for "What's In It For Me?" It is pronounced "wiffum." This is the question each audience member asks consciously (or unconsciously) when a speaker starts talking. Although audiences may believe they are motivated by worthy and altruistic causes, they usually want to learn how to get rich, look younger, become more knowledgeable or advance their careers.

If you understand these typical human needs and address the ones which are crucially important for your listeners, they will sit up and pay attention. The sooner you accomplish this, the better. I call it

Instant Rapport

How can you achieve Instant Rapport? Talk to your audience about themselves. Yes, I know it is your financial plan or R&D's new project, but the sooner you mention how it will improve their lives, the sooner they will listen.

Eliminate the word "I." Use the word "you." Not "I have a great vision" but "Without you, our vision will fail." You. You. You. Music to their ears.

What if you have a pertinent message but the timing is awful? Peter Boller of Converium was asked to give his updated actuarial report at a Friday afternoon meeting (scheduled by someone else). We all know that Friday afternoon is one of the worst times to engage an audience. What did Peter do? He strode briskly to the front of the auditorium, looked at the audience of 180 people and said, "Good afternoon…(pause)…Friday afternoon." His audience responded audibly. Half of them chuckled; the other half moaned. Then Peter gave his report. Everyone listened because he had acknowledged what was going on in their heads. Instant Rapport in four words!

How can you maintain the rapport? By constantly assessing your audience and adapting as you go along. The first time I delivered my keynote address "Green Light Your Life," I said, "You need to figure out where **your** talents and the **world's** needs meet. That is where you will find your destiny." Big word, destiny.

As soon as I said it, the mood in the room changed. Instead of continuing, I paused and repeated the statement slowly because I sensed that everyone was making a quick mental assessment, "What are my talents? What are the world's needs? Where do they meet? What is my destiny?" Now I know that I need to pause after I say the word "destiny." We need these moments in our speeches. Yes, in the business world. They happen when we touch the audience's WIIFM.

Although I use the word "audience" throughout *Speaking Globally*, when you are determining your objectives, you need to think of your audience as individuals instead of some amorphous entity. Each person in your audience has her own concerns, his special expectations. When you prepare your speech, try to see these different faces in your mind's eye and make sure your message reaches every single one of them.

30 Minutes × 200 People = 100 Hours of Persuasion

A lot of speakers begrudge the effort that goes into preparing and delivering a 30-minute speech to an audience of 200. But think of it this way: if you had to give your message to one person after another, the half-hours would add up quickly. You would need 100 hours to get your message across. If you get it right, a 30-minute speech is an efficient way to communicate. That is why you need to know as much as possible about each of those 200 people.

You probably have a general idea of who will be in your audience, but find out as much as you can before you start preparing your speech. Ask the person who has invited you to tell you about your audience or get in touch with some previous speakers. Another way to learn about your audience is to ask the organizers for the names of delegates and contact several of them by phone. Introduce yourself and ask why they will be attending your presentation. Explain that you want to be sure to concentrate on the issues which are of interest to them.

To guide you in your research, look at the Audience Research Questions given in Figure 1.2 on p. 7. You should be able to answer all of them before you begin writing your speech.

On the day of your presentation, no matter how much advance information you have, make a point of arriving early to get acquainted with your audience. Introduce yourself. Find out how they like the conference so far. This is an excellent opportunity to gauge the prevailing mood of the audience, and you may learn something which you can use in your presentation.

Since you will not have a first-hand look at your audience until you begin speaking, this preparatory work will get you started on the right track. You need to start where your audience is in order to take them to your destination which is, of course, your "desired end result."

FIGURE 1.2 Audience research questions

AUDIENCE RESEARCH QUESTIONS

1. What does this audience want to know?

2. What do they need to know?

3. What will convince them?
   Information _____
   Facts and figures _____
   Personal testimonials _____

4. How will you know if you have succeeded?

5. Are they attending voluntarily?

6. Will any decision-makers be present?

7. What is this audience's perception of you?
   An expert _____
   An adversary _____
   An unknown _____

8. Initially, what attitude will this audience have towards your subject and your organization?
   Receptive _____
   Neutral _____
   Hostile _____

9. Are there any local customs or prejudices to be aware of?

10. What is this audience's WIIFM?

CHAPTER

Design a
Winning Speech

FIGURE 2.1 "My speech"

Choosing the best framework for your speech will make it easier to determine your main points and to remember them. This chapter gives you guidelines on choosing a format. Of course, most of us have a preferred way of organizing material, but it is useful to have other structures in our repertoire.

You have probably seen this "generic" speech outline. Simple and concise, it does make a point!

The "Tell Them" Technique

❧ First you tell them what you're going to tell them.

❧ Then you tell them.

❧ Finally you tell them what you have told them.

Choose an Appropriate Format: Seven Ways to Organize Your Speech

What's crucial is that your format helps both you and your audience keep tabs of where you are in the grand scheme of things. In a book, you can turn back a page to refresh your memory or look ahead to see what's coming. In a speech you have to be able to accomplish this verbally.

1. Chronological

This is the easiest way to organize a talk because it's the way we live our lives: past, present, future. German audiences appreciate historical background so this is a good format to use with them. For variation, you can begin in the present tense and then flash back to the past.

Today Integrated Sprockets International has 12,000 full-time employees located in four countries. We currently produce 1,200 sprocket types which we distribute to 67 countries around the globe. A century ago, we were a gleam in the eye of Mr. Charles Tibbitts, an enterprising mechanical genius from the Rattlesnake Hills. Let's go back to 1904 and trace an amazing success story. In the beginning . . .

2. Spatial

You divide your subject matter into geographical regions. Begin with the head office in Beijing, then talk about the regional offices in China and finally discuss your 12 other offices around the globe.

3. The List

This is the format to choose if you want to list your main points as lists, categories or topics.

> Three major types of change in the environment can produce conflict:
>
> 1. Natural catastrophes, such as floods and earthquakes.
>
> 2. Changes by large engineering actions, such as dam-building and mining.
>
> 3. Changes resulting from the cumulative effects of large numbers of small actions, such as land clearing and dumping waste into the water.

The way you order the points depends upon what you want to emphasize. At an environmental symposium, Professor Kurt Spillmann of the Federal Institute of Technology in Zurich chose this order because he wanted to concentrate on the final point: how individual actions have unintended and negative effects.

Limit yourself to three or four points. If you announce that you have "25 Ways to Improve Listening Skills," no one will listen. Instead, cluster your tips into three categories: "How to Listen at Conferences, in the Office and at Home." Audiences like "how to" lists, as long as they are manageable.

4. The Acronym

An acronym is a word formed from the initial letters of several words. Examples in English include "snafu" (systems normal, all fouled up), "posh" (port out, starboard home) and from German "flak" Fl(ieger) a(bwehr) k(anone), which means anti-aircraft fire. It's a catchy way for an audience to remember your message!

> When Dick King was corporate vice-president of Electronic Data Services (EDS), he hosted a meeting for senior management in Geneva.

In his presentation, he explained how his people were:

1. **A**dding value to customers,

2. **L**everaging products and services, and

3. **P**roviding trans-national solutions to reach EDS's

4. **S**trategic intent.

He began by saying: "Welcome to Switzerland! Isn't that a spectacular view of the snow-capped Alps as you fly in to Geneva? Most of the time I'm also seeing them from the sky, but I like to spend my weekends exploring those mountains. I've learned you don't just start climbing. First you have to figure precisely which route to take to reach the summit. That's exactly what we are doing with our business plan."

Dick explained how by **A**dding value, **L**everaging, and **P**roviding transnational solutions, his unit would achieve their **S**trategic intent. His final slide showed the acronym **ALPS**. In addition, everyone received a Plexiglas topographical model of the Matterhorn.

FIGURE 2.2 The ALPS slide

5. Comparison/Contrast

When you compare two things, you show what they have in common. When you contrast, you point out differences.

In a speech at The China Summit, Dr. Seung-Soo Han, Deputy Prime Minister of the Republic of Korea compared the independent development of China and Korea since the 1960s, including their agrarian beginnings, their industrialization, their open-door policies and their recognition that modern global economic order demands interdependency and open exchanges among nations. The comparisons stressed the similarity between Korea and China and made a convincing case for a strong "emerging partnership" between the two nations.

6. Analogy

An analogy compares one thing to another. The formula is A *is like* B. For example, "Learning to speak is like learning to swim. You can learn the techniques and even practice on dry land, but eventually you have to dive in and get wet!"

In a speech at a technical symposium sponsored by the paper industry, Stephen Oliver compared a revolutionary new line of polymers to a game of pool. His colorful slides included a pool table with solid and striped balls symbolizing the polymers' chemistry and applications. For his conclusion, he actually pulled an eight ball out of his pocket and said, "If you choose our products, you will be a winner." This may seem like a bit of a gimmick, but Stephen wanted prospective buyers to remember him, and they did!

7. Problem-Solution

Mayor Richard M. Daley kicked off the first-ever North American Greening Rooftops Conference by stating that cities have environmental problems, including "too much concrete and steel and not enough green space. When people talk about the environment, we usually think of Alaska. But here in Chicago, we are committed to improving our environment." Then succinctly, he explained how Chicago solves problems. "We've planted 300,000 trees. We've built more than 60 miles of landscaped medians, complete with drainage systems—more than in any other US city. We're protecting our Lake Michigan shoreline. And we are hosting this conference because we know that Green Roofs are part of the solution. Our first project was putting a rooftop garden on City Hall to improve air quality and save energy. It is such a success that we've added bees. Now we have honey atop City Hall! With 43 Green Roof projects throughout the city, we are committed to making Chicago the greenest city in the country."

Sources for Material

For many business speeches, your information will come from company resources. However, you may need additional material to help convey your message, prove your point, add credibility or brighten up your speech. For more information about using appropriate stories, please refer to Chapter 4. Sources of information include:

- 🐝 Your local research librarian (if you are lucky enough to have one).

- 🐝 Internet sources.

- 🐝 The research departments of newspapers and television stations.

- 🐝 Experts. (Call or send a letter requesting ten minutes of their valuable time. If you tickle their WIIFM, you will usually get your interview.)

In the meantime, the following guidelines will make your hard facts more palatable.

Dealing with Data: Limit, Simplify, Sequence

Limit Your Data

Resist sharing all your facts and figures with your audience. Pick only the juiciest plums from the tree. In your speech, stress the first, largest, smallest, latest or newest. If you need to give your audience complex formulations or detailed sets of figures, announce during your speech that the information will be available afterwards.

In a speech in South Africa, Cees Geel showed a transparency overcrowded with data. Immediately he turned off the overhead projector, smiled at his audience and said, "I realize you couldn't read those figures. That is why I have prepared a wall chart for each of you with an overview of our solvents with their physical properties." He held up a large colorful poster and added, "There is a chart for each of you on the back table. When I visit you, I hope to see it hanging on your wall."

Stick to the Magic Rule of Three: Groups of three are easily remembered, such as "healthy, wealthy and wise," and "see no evil, hear no evil, speak no evil." Lists of three are good for repetition, for emphasis and for speech titles. If you incorporate alliteration (repeating the same sound at the beginning of the words), retention increases:

🕮 The Body Shop promotes refilling, reusing and recycling.

🕮 "Grazing, Garage Sales and Gratitude: A Light-hearted Look at American Life." This is the title of a speech of mine.

Simplify Your Data

🕮 *Tweak just a tad:* Nigeria has 129,934,911 inhabitants. Round it up and say "almost 130 million inhabitants."

🕮 *Repeat and rephrase numbers:* If you say, "Our sales were 30 percent more than our competitor's sales," it helps to add, "That's three–zero." (You don't want your audience to hear 13 percent, do you?)

🕮 *Humanize your numbers:*
  – Version 1: You say, "We need to save paper. Last year at headquarters, we used 580,000 sheets of paper a day." Your audience thinks, "So what!"
  – Version 2: You say, "We need to save paper. Let's aim for a 10 percent reduction. Last year each of you used an average of 212 sheets of paper a day." Your audience thinks, "Wow! I can save 21 sheets of paper a day."

Sequence Your Data

🕮 Bridge from *known territory to the unknown,* from the *simple to complex.* "Let us begin with exchange rates before discussing arbitrage."

❁ Move from areas of *mutual agreement* to those of disagreement. This is particularly useful when dealing with a hostile or negative audience. "Let us first discuss the areas where we have reached agreement, which are quality control, labeling and pricing." Then continue, "Now let us discuss distribution rights."

❁ Go from *less to more* (or from more to less) but keep it consistent. "We will first have a look at our economy model and then move up the line to the luxury edition."

Check for Accuracy

Only use up-to-date and reliable resources.

Give Credit Where Credit Is Due

Quote your sources and do your best to track down the correct author. If you cannot locate a source, admit it. For example: "I was unable to find out who said that 'Great Britain and the United States are nations separated by a common language.'" (It was George Bernard Shaw.)

Facts and Figures Impress, but Passion Persuades

Passion is in short supply in the business world, the scientific world and the academic world — at least on the speaker's platform. Passion need not express itself in emotional outbursts. Passion can be quietly intense. It signals to the audience that you care about your message and that they should, too.

Three Ways to Write Your Speech: Stringing, Molding and Juggling

A speech can only be delivered in one order: You start at the beginning, then you move to the middle and you end up at the conclusion. Isn't that a relief? You can, however, prepare a speech in a variety of ways.

1. If you take the string of pearls approach, you begin by writing down the first word you will say and then systematically proceeding until you finish with the final word, like stringing pearls on a thread.

2. If you prefer delving into the facts, figures and other materials which comprise the middle of your speech, first create the "meatloaf" (or main course) before dealing with the starter or the dessert — that is, the introduction and conclusion of your speech.

3. You may work on all three parts of a speech simultaneously: honing an opening anecdote, checking out supporting evidence and preparing a powerful ending. That's like juggling three balls in the air.

However you choose to complete this process, your ideas should eventually fall into an arrangement that makes sense. Now put your speech away for at least 24 hours — but preferably one week. Then take a long hard look at what you have written. If you record your speeches into a Dictaphone like I do instead of writing them out, listen to the tape and take notes. This distance gives you objectivity you need to weed out extraneous material or rephrase fuzzy ideas.

Use Large Cards for Your Notes

Unless you have a photographic memory or a very brief speech, you will need notes to keep you on track. Use 4" × 6" cards (rather than full-size pages) — they force you to be concise and don't flutter in your hands. You can also keep them in your inside pocket (women need a jacket with large pockets) and pull them out only if you need them. No need to make a big show or apologize. Act as if you had planned on referring to your notes at that point. Hold them up so you can see what you have written. Don't use little cards or try to conceal them in the palm of your hand.

If the conference organizers want your speech for the interpreters or for distribution afterwards, send them your written speech but don't feel obligated to use it on the day.

You may start out with a large stack of cards but each time you run through your speech, you can condense the notes. The fewer cards you have, the less shuffling you have to do. Personally, I limit myself to two cards which I place side by side on the lectern. Then I needn't pick them up. I just "wander" over for a quick check or to scoop up a date.

Here's my card for a speech to the BPW International XXIVth Congress in Melbourne, Australia. It may make little sense to you, but each point reminded me of what I wanted to say.

FIGURE 2.3 Cue card for a speech to BPW

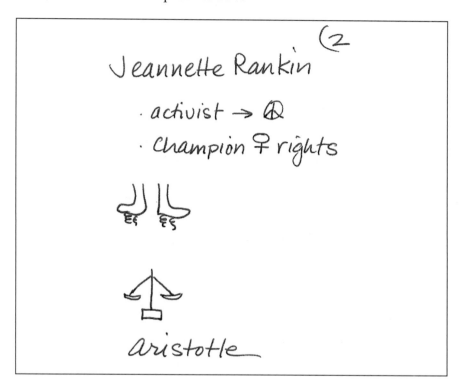

Suggestions for Your Note Cards

⏺ Choose high prompt words:

1. — the name Jeannette Rankin cued me to say that my second cousin, the first woman elected to US Congress, voted "no" to entry into both World Wars.

2 "activist for peace" and "champion women's rights" helped me say those exact phrases.

3. Whenever possible, draw icons to encompass an entire idea. The feet with roots symbolize being grounded. The scales stand for the balance between speaker and audience. Of course, when I want to remember Aristotle, it's easier to write his name than to draw a Greek orator stick figure.

❦ Print large and use only one side of card.

❦ If you have more than one, number the cards.

❦ Don't change the cards, once you have set your speech.

❦ Do make a photocopy, in case you misplace your originals.

❦ Use color for emphasis: red for dates, green for transition words, etc.

❦ Use arrows, a happy face (smile!), draw pictures, a large P = Pause.

Include Signpost Words

You may find it useful to add specific transition words to your note cards. Particularly when you are in a multi-lingual speaking situation, these linking words are valuable to tell your listener where you have been, where you are and where you are headed.

Examples:

Addition: and, besides, furthermore, in addition, moreover, finally.

Contrast: but, and yet, however, in spite of, in contrast to this, nevertheless, not, on the contrary, whereas.

Alternative: or, not, otherwise, neither nor, on the other hand.

Consequence: therefore, hence, consequently, accordingly, under such circumstances, as a result.

Once you have chosen a format, selected your data, composed your speech and prepared speaker notes, the major part of your job is over, right? Wrong! You still need to create visuals and practice your speech out loud. But you are now well on your way. At least you know what you want to say!

3

Begin and End Dynamically

Amidst polite applause, a silver-haired portly man walks to the front of the room. As he mounts the steps, he drops his manuscript and scurries to pick up the scattered pages. Then he moves behind the huge lectern and without even glancing at the audience begins reading in a monotonous voice. After five seconds, several voices call from the back of the room, "Your microphone isn't on."

As the speaker fumbles for the switch, a sound technician appears and reaches into the speaker's ample waistline for the battery pack.

"Shit! These damn microphones!" are the speaker's first words to echo through the large auditorium.

An audience gives you anywhere from seven to 15 seconds to establish credibility. After which they decide whether to stay tuned in or switch off. That's why you need to choose your opening words more carefully than Mr. Portly did!

The time required to create forceful introductory and concluding remarks is well invested. Where is our attention level highest? What do we remember best? Where do the television crews congregate? At the starting point and finish line of the race. When are we most involved? When the curtain goes up and at the final moment before it comes down. What dates do we remember? Birth and death.

Beginnings

Six Ways to Begin Dynamically

1. Connect with your audience by mentioning them and their country.

At Dow's First Paint Seminar in Poland, Peter Drew began: "On my first visit to Warsaw as we were driving to the hotel, I saw a vendor along the side of the road selling cans of paint. Now I have traveled all over Europe, but I had never seen that before. It made a great impression. At that very moment, I decided that Poland would be one of our important areas in paint development. That is why we are here today."

Well done! In just 20 seconds, Peter got his audience's attention, made a connection and gave them a valid reason for listening: their future together.

Martin Grob of Finanz AG spoke in several cities to profile his organization's activities. Although it was his first stay in the United States, he knew that each city would appreciate a few special words.

In Chicago, he said, "Chicago's a great city, but a little confusing for us foreigners. Can anyone tell me why you have the statue of Lincoln in Grant Park and the statue of Grant in Lincoln Park?"

In San Francisco, Martin began, "I came to New York last September but only now I am making the trip from 'sea to shining sea.'"

His audiences appreciated his "localized" touches and made a point of telling him so.

2. Tell a personal anecdote.

Although most business people avoid references to their private lives, it is a useful device for letting your audience see that you are human. Besides which, only speakers who feel comfortable and in control share personal experiences. So, if you want to generate an aura of command, tell a story.

Martin Grob began his talk with a true story: "Four years ago, my fiancée and I were in a remote Egyptian village on the Sinai peninsula. While running on the beach, she tripped and sprained her ankle. Back at the guest house, we applied ice but when the swelling didn't go down, we decided to see a doctor. The doctor himself was unshaven and bleary eyed. The consulting room was dark and shabby.

The set-up didn't inspire a lot of confidence. After looking at her ankle, he opened his medicine cabinet. It was filled with medicine from Swiss firms like Hoffmann-LaRoche and Sandoz. We realized we were closer to civilization than we had thought. The medicine worked wonders, and her ankle recovered. The question remains: how did all these pharmaceuticals get to Egypt and who paid for them? Quite possibly my company Finanz AG financed this transaction. Let me tell you about our activities."

If you think Martin's story went on too long, it is because you are reading his story. In reality, his audiences listened with interest. They were curious as to why he was telling them such a story—until he made his point, that is.

3. Ask a pertinent question.

"Are you a good networker?" is how Elaine Ferré began her talk to an international group of business women. Then she said, "Do you know the person next to you? Well, introduce yourself. That's how networking starts!"

Simple and effective.

4. Use a visual prop or gimmick.

A tall well-built man walked to the front of the room with a heavy bag over his shoulder. He looked at the audience and dropped the bag on the floor. It made a loud resounding thump. Then he said, "That bag of firewood weighs 50 pounds. That's how much weight I lost by changing my eating habits. If you would like to change a habit, let me give you some suggestions."

That bag of firewood made the point. The audience saw it, heard it and could easily imagine lugging it around.

5. Do something unexpected.

Cheri Lofland, then head of Group Communications for Reckitt & Colman, mounted the steps to the stage and then walked across the long stage looking at the audience, but not saying a word. She turned and repeated the process until she reached center stage. She smiled

An appropriate prop makes a strong statement.

and said, "Even though I have not yet said one word, we've been communicating for the last 20 seconds."

Then Cheri began her presentation on how to use verbal and non-verbal communication when dealing with customers.

6. Involve your audience.

Betty Zucker, management consultant and author, cannot speak above a whisper so she begins by saying, "You don't need to worry about my voice. I don't have laryngitis, and it doesn't hurt me to talk this way. This is just my voice. In fact, it has become my logo, but it does require careful listening. Of course, for you in management, good listening is a basic skill, so I am not worried."

What does this approach do? It makes her listeners responsible for concentrating on her message instead being concerned about her voice. Inevitably, her audiences rise to the challenge! Wouldn't you?!

Tell Your Audience Why They Should Listen to You

Once you have grabbed your audience's attention and forged a connection, you need to let them know that you will be worth listening to! It is not the same as telling them what you are talking about.

If you say, "I'm going to tell you about our environmentally friendly solvents," your audience thinks: "So what."

If you say, "Our new line of solvents already meets the EU requirements which will be mandatory by 2010," your audience thinks: "Hmm, my solvents won't meet those new laws. This could be something for me."

Six Ways Not to Begin Your Presentation

1. Don't start with an apology.
Speaking at the United Nations Environment Program, an Italian financial adviser planned to begin with an apology for her less than perfect English. She was dissuaded from such an approach, and you should be, too. Audiences are grateful if you are speaking in their language or a language which they understand. They will readily forgive a mistake or an accented pronunciation if you just get on with your message.

2. Don't tell your audience you are unprepared.

> An arrogant banker (not a client of mine) began a talk to a woman's organization: "I didn't have time to prepare, but I hope my words will be like a miniskirt: short enough to keep your attention and long enough to cover the essentials."

What a double-barreled insult. Needless to say, his presentation was not a success.

3. Eschew platitudes.

> "Good morning, ladies and gentlemen. It is a pleasure to be here. Today I would like to take a few minutes of your time to discuss a subject of importance to me and you. It is an important issue. Not only important to those of us in the room but to people around the world."

What did we learn? Nothing. How long did we listen? Almost 30 seconds. Leave the blah, blah, blah to the politicians.

4. Avoid questionable humor.

At a financial management meeting in Antwerp, the morning's four speakers sat in the front of a large conference room. The first two men spoke in British English. Next a Puerto Rican analyst spoke in fluent English which was lightly accented. Finally, a Canadian (not a client of mine) walked to the lectern and began, "Congratulations! I am the first speaker this morning who is speaking to you without an accent." The audience gasped audibly, and the temperature in the room dropped several degrees. Although he had grabbed their attention with his attempt at humor, he had alienated the entire audience.

So, get the attention of your audience but not at the expense of anyone in the room.

5. Never begin in the dark.
It's impossible to establish a connection if your audience cannot see you.

The marketing director of an international airline started her speech by showing a specially-made video welcoming her audience on board a flight. This clever introduction backfired because the audience could not see her. Even worse, no one turned the lights up after her video, so she stayed in the dark.

6. Never avoid the issue that is on everyone's mind.
The day before the president of a major industrial firm spoke in London, headlines announced the unexpected departure of his entire legal staff. He scrapped his planned introduction and began,

As I stand here, I can imagine what is on your minds. You'd like to know more about the story which hit the press yesterday. Since our departing attorneys and we have signed an agreement of non-disclosure, it's impossible for me to discuss details at this time. For me, it's a little like that expression, "damned if you do, damned if you don't." Now before I begin my prepared speech, let me add that I will happily take questions at the conclusion, with the exception of any dealing with this issue.

What had he done? He had faced a controversial issue head on and preempted any questions at the end of his speech. He showed that he was human and in control.

Who Comes Up with First-Rate Openers?

Usually you do! It may be the result of concerted effort, but it's often an offhand remark you make. What you need is someone like me who pounces on possible material and asks questions: "How much weight did you lose?" or "Why were you in Egypt?"

If you don't have someone to ask you probing questions, just start listening to yourself and collecting your own comments. Jot your ideas into a notebook or use a Dictaphone.

And when you brainstorm, don't be judgmental! Be magnanimous and give yourself permission to think "outside the boxes." Just imagine if Wilbur Wright had said to his brother Orville, "Fly?"

In deciding how you want to begin, mentally check every possible introductory idea from your audience's perspective. What you might find inconsequential could be meaningful to your audience. As you read earlier, Martin Grob touched a chord by quoting the phrase "from sea to shining sea," which is from America the Beautiful. Peter Drew did it by mentioning paint cans in Poland. These openers were attention-getters which made the audience say, "This person took some time and effort to learn a little about us. If he has taken as much care with his message, then we are in for a treat."

Endings

Your ending is your "last chance" to get your audience's attention. As studies have shown, audiences perk up their ears as soon as they hear the melodious phrase, "In conclusion." Your ending is the perfect place to accomplish three things:

1. Summarize your key points.

2. Activate your audience.

3. Leave them wanting more.

First of all, you need to review the main points of your presentation. Do it briefly and with energy:

Let's summarize what we did: First we added value, second we lever-aged our products and services, and then we provided transnational solutions. By focusing on these three priorities, we were able to reach our strategic intent.

Second, you need to activate your audience to accomplish your desired end result. To "fly, buy, or try." I suggested in the last chapter that you create your ending first. The sooner you create it, the sooner you can use it as a standard to measure each and every thing that goes into your speech. If an argument, a quotation or an anecdote does not help you reach your goal, discard it (or put it aside for another presentation.)

That is why I encourage you to create your ending early in the planning stages when you are bubbling over with fresh ideas and enthusiasm. Once you have coined your riveting words, memorize them word for word! Then no matter what happens during your talk or how off course you get, you will have a safe place to aim for.

"Leave your audience wanting more" is an old show-business adage. Your conclusion should be brief, powerful and final. Unfortunately, many speeches in the business world have endings which are lengthy, weak and inconclusive. To make sure that this chapter ends with a bang, not a whim-per, let's get the "how not to endings" over with first.

Four Ways Not to End Your Speech

1. Don't end with "Thank you."
It is customary, and many business speakers conclude with "Thank you" because it does send a clear signal to your audience — kind of like a Pavlovian bell that rings, "You can wake up now." Unfortunately, it is a ter-rible waste of the best spot in your speech. You need to choose words which are gripping and strong.

Besides which, saying "Thank you" isn't logical. Why would you thank your audience? You are the one who has planned and practiced. You are the one who has prepared some colorful slides and bought a new suit. You are the one who has had butterflies in your stomach. All the audience has to do is show up. As Woody Allen once said, "Ninety percent of life is just show-ing up." Your audience should be thanking you.

2. Don't end with an announcement.
If you are asked to make an announcement about the coffee break, insert it

like this, "Before I wrap up, let me remind you that coffee will be served on the terrace today. Now, in conclusion . . ."

3. Don't end by asking, "What questions may I answer?"

Some speakers bridge directly from their prepared speeches into questions and answers without even taking a breath. Making a distinction between your prepared speech and the Question and Answer (Q&A) session makes good sense. First you give your final message twice: first in its "proper place" and then again at the end of the discussion session. That's right. At the very end, you say, "I have certainly appreciated the opportunity to introduce our financial product. Your lively comments and probing questions are proof that we're headed in the right direction with our Shop and Swap Bonds."

4. Don't end by saying, "In conclusion" and then not concluding.

Endings are tough. In speeches, as well as in real life. Far too many speakers just do not know how to get those final words out. They wander farther and farther down the path of indecisiveness hoping against hope that someone or something will intervene. These are the same people who linger at your front door after a dinner party and cannot bring themselves to say "good night" and leave.

Provide what you promise. Make your conclusion concise and clear. Even if they have not followed your entire speech, most listeners will tune in to capture a good take-home message. Don't disappoint them.

The Right Way to Finish in First Place!

Think of the ending of your speech like the finale of a symphony. All the stops are out. The notes are strong and determined. Your ending should be resolute, too. In fact, if you do a consummate job, your audience should sit for a moment in stunned silence before breaking into resounding applause.

Yes, I know you are giving a business speech in a conference hall not a recital in a concert hall, but you still need to aim for that ending with everything you have. The last words out of your mouth are the most important words you utter because they have the best chance of being remembered.

The most elegant and satisfying way to end your speech is to refer back to your beginning. In his speech to EDS managers, Dick King began by talking about the magnificent Swiss Alps and mountain climbing. In his conclusion he returned to his analogy to illustrate how his group had reached the summit.

In addition to choosing the right words, you need to position them in the optimal order and then pronounce them with resolution. It all adds up to maximum impact.

Version Number 1:   "Working together, we can ensure that we will become more successful as the years go by."

Version Number 2:   "Working together, we can ensure the future success of Uni-world."

The second sentence is shorter, and your company name is in the "place of honor." Naturally, the way you say the final sentence makes a difference. In most cases you will want to slow down and drop the pitch of your voice. Articulate carefully. Once the final word is out of your mouth, pause grandly. Let your audience see by the expression on your face that you are indeed finished. Remember your body language communicates as strongly as your words.

If you want to say "thank you," do it now but as an afterthought. Don't let it substitute for that strong final sentence. If you do memorize your final sentence, then no matter what happens in the course of your speech you can finish with a flourish.

Variation: If you are urging your audience to "storm the barricades" in order to reach your desired end reaction, your final sentence needs to thrust upward and onward with mounting fervor. Start waving your rhetorical banner with a well-chosen rallying cry like "Time is running out." Then with increasing pitch and pulsating emotion, voice your final sentence, "Working together, we can ensure the future success of Uni-world."

When I am on the speaker's circuit, I talk about communication. My final sentence is a fitting way to conclude this chapter:

"If you take a positive approach, prepare thoroughly and practice out loud, you will find unlimited opportunities to speak for yourself!"

4

Make Your
Message Memorable

Max Robinson decided to open a one-day chemical conference in the Czech Republic on a personal note to let his audience know how pleased he was to be in their country. He began, "As a boy, I played the clarinet in my school orchestra. My favorite music was the New World Symphony. However, I never dreamt that one day I would be speaking in the country where Dvorak was born." Then Max mentioned the Czech Nobel Prize winners and his love for Czech beer—the "original" Budweiser. By adding a personal touch, Max helped make his speech memorable.

Of course, you will be remembered if you tumble off the platform or split open your trousers. The unexpected and the embarrassing can be counted on to get the job done. Let's concentrate in this chapter on more positive ways to make a lasting impression. First, position yourself differently from the other speakers. Second, add a personal touch.

Position Yourself Differently from the Other Speakers

When you receive an invitation to speak, find out who else will be on the program. If the conference is about Opportunities in Asia, and you are the only speaker from the consumer goods sector, your position is secured. If, on the other hand, the conference is focusing on Asian Opportunities for Fast Moving Consumer Goods (FMCG), you need to determine how your audience will remember that you are from Procter and Gamble and not Unilever.

Certainly your message and the logo on your slides are important, but you can profile yourself in other ways, too.

Use Your Natural Advantages

If the conference is filled with silver-haired executives, and you are a 30-year old sales director, don't don a stern demeanor. Let your youthfulness add zest and energy to the agenda.

If you speak with an accent, don't try to change it. And do not apologize for it. Your voice is one of your distinguishing features. Do, however, begin slowly. Very slowly. Your audience requires at least one minute to adjust to your speech pattern. Then if you articulate clearly and project your voice, you will be understood. During your speech, keep a lookout to gauge how you are coming across. If you have any doubts, repeat a sentence.

Unfortunately, women are in the minority at the speaker's lectern. Use that to your advantage. Chapter 10 has been written with you in mind.

Dare to Be Different

Speak without slides.
If all the speakers are using slides, speak without any. (Obviously you will determine this in advance.)

> A marketing director once began a talk, "You can close your eyes now because I don't have any slides. But I hope you'll keep your ears open because my message is worth hearing." Needless to say, the audience kept ears and eyes open!

Do it with your wardrobe.
As the Country Profiles show, the accepted dress code in the international business world is usually a suit. Sometimes, however, the rules may be relaxed.

> When a Belgian attorney speaking at a resort hotel in West Virginia learned the dress code was casual, he decided not to comply. Standing in front of the audience dressed in a polo shirt and khaki pants, he would have felt uncomfortable. He wore a jacket and tie and explained, "Since you want me to compare the European and the American approach to international dispute resolution, here is a visual cue: we take a formal approach."

However, not following suit can backfire.

> An American professor participated in a conference in Hamburg wearing a polo shirt, khaki trousers and loafers. The other 400 participants wore suits. Oblivious to the dress code, he wondered why he was ignored during the panel discussion.

When in doubt about what to wear, it is preferable to take a conservative approach, unless fashion is your forte.

> A top executive in the Italian fashion industry discovered on the way up to the stage that he was wearing one black shoe and one brown shoe. His presentation was an overwhelming success. Now whenever he has a major speech, he wears mismatched footwear. (And he tells the audience. They love it!)

React on the Spot

Dealing with the dynamics of the conference room can also give you a powerful edge over the majority of speakers. If the audience is squinting because the afternoon sun is shining into their eyes, you can say: "Let's close those blinds a little so people can see better."

When you make a reference to a previous speaker, your credibility will skyrocket with your audience. "As we heard earlier from the Malaysian Prime Minister, we need to develop a set of principles to form the basis for coordinating investment policies. Let me suggest how the private sector can contribute . . ."

Given the choice, always stand up to speak. You have better visibility and more energy. You may have to seize the opportunity. At one session of the World Economic Forum Summit in Hong Kong, five speakers were seated in the front of the room. The first three speakers remained seated in low slung back chairs as they discussed the future of Thailand. The fourth speaker, extricated himself from his chair saying, "I think I will stretch my legs" as he walked to the lectern to speak. Clever fellow!

However, if the other speakers are standing up, you should not sit down! You will lose valuable visibility. You could, however, move into the audience to ask them a question. (If a microphone is necessary, you will need a cordless one.)

You can be the "shortest" speaker. At a school awards day, more than 2,000 students, faculty and family were packed into a stuffy auditorium. All the speakers ran overtime. Finally the superintendent of schools stood up and said, "You have already heard enough speeches on this hot and sticky day. You won't remember anything from my 30-minute prepared talk, but you might remember me for saying just one word: Congratulations!" He sat down. We gave him a standing ovation. And I do remember!

Personalize Your Message

If you say, "On the way here from the airport" or "As I reached for my passport," your audience perks up their ears and pays attention. No matter where you are on the face of the planet, as you begin telling a story your audience gets involved. They enjoy themselves, they learn and they remember. So do not depend exclusively on charts and fourth quarter reports to get your message across. Tell a story!

> The board of ABB (Asea Brown Boveri) summoned George Lercher from his post on the island of Java to give a progress report. Although Mr. Lercher had been with the firm for many years, he had never met a single board member. He had never delivered a speech, and he was asked to speak in English, instead of his native Swiss-German.
>
> Mr. Lercher had, however, seen business presentations, so he prepared a 45-minute talk supported by 60 transparencies. At his first rehearsal, which I videotaped, he spoke in a soft voice and kept his hands in his pockets when he wasn't changing transparencies.
>
> When I asked him about Java, Mr. Lercher's face lit up, and he replied, "It's another world. We moved in 10 months ago with all the latest telecommunications equipment, but we soon realized that something was wrong. Deliveries were not being made, and supplies were not arriving on schedule. When I investigated, I learned that the local people were miffed by our way of communicating. They were used to getting letters, with signatures, delivered to them by messengers on scooters."
>
> When I asked, "What did you do?" he continued, "I had to solve the problem. I got some messengers and scooters. We signed the orders with a fountain pen and had them hand delivered. It was amazing. Once we adapted to their way of communicating, the deliveries started coming in right on time."

When I suggested that he tell this to his Board of Directors, Mr. Lercher replied, "Oh, I couldn't tell them a story. I am giving a business talk."

With a little coaxing and a little coaching, he did tell the story to his international board of directors, who learned from their man on the scene what can happen when two cultures meet face-to-face.

And isn't it interesting that as soon as ABB started personalizing their messages, they got better results?

Let a story help deliver your message.

Look inside Your Life

If you are not sure where to find an appropriate story, just look inside your life. Often the material for an anecdote may be staring you in the face.

I worked with a man whose office walls were covered with huge road maps. When I asked him why, he explained, "I am from Chicago, and we never learned much geography in school. In fact, when I was transferred to Paris, I wasn't even sure where Brussels was in relation to Bruges, so I bought a map and tacked it up. When I started traveling to Kazakhstan and Uzbekistan, I hung up another map. Now my company is ready to expand into Africa and India. More maps! I'm learning geography and decorating my office at the same time."

He began his speech to his board of directors by saying, "When you visit me in Paris, you'll see that my office is wallpapered with maps." Then he explained why. You see, he wanted a go-ahead for expansion into new areas that his board had never heard of, much less visited. By admitting that he once had difficulties in distinguishing one foreign place from another, he built a bond with his audience. Did I mention his board meeting was in Chicago?

Even a brief comment will liven things up if it lets your audience paint a picture in their minds and gives them a glimpse of the man behind the corporate mask.

In the middle of a talk bulging with facts and figures, the president of a multi-national industrial firm disclosed, "I love landing in a city like Kuala Lumpur where I can see lots of building cranes. That is a sure sign the city is growing. And that is a place where we want to be."

Reveal Something Personal

A speaker who divulges a little bit about him or herself is a person in power, especially if the anecdote includes an admission of fallibility. Listen to Dr. René Imhof, discussing the results of his 360 degree assessment with his staff of 1200 people:

"You know what I learned? I spend too much time thinking and creating in an 'ivory tower.' Typical for us scientists! But as the Head of Pharma Research Basel at Roche, I need to 'walk the talk.' Right now, I may not be walking, but I sure am talking. I like working in teams and being with good people like you, but it may not always show. So I am learning to let you see my passion. I encourage you to recognize and switch your passion on, too."

Especially if you are not the boss, include a little anecdote in your next speech. Adding a personal touch sends a powerful signal. Your audience reasons, "If this speaker can let a little of herself shine through in such a confident manner, she must feel very comfortable and in control of her job, too. She's going places."

Start collecting your own anecdotes. Jot your ideas down or record them on your Dictaphone. Before long you will have your own personal reference library of rich and vivid examples to accompany you up the ladder of success.

Storytime! Find the Story in Your Message

Remember a "you won't believe what happened to me" true story with a lesson to be learned which could be incorporated into a business talk. Suggestions to tease your memory:

- ❂ your first job interview

- ❂ your most embarrassing experience

- ❂ a travel mishap (flight canceled, lost hotel reservation)

- ❂ a crisis — losing money, getting lost

- ❂ a story about growing up in your native land

Relate the crucial facts:

- ❂ Who _____

- ❂ What _____

- ❂ Where _____

- ❂ When _____

- ❂ Why _____

If you start with the words "Imagine this!" or "Let me set the scene," everyone in your audience will switch into "story mode." Then you need to involve their senses.

In one of my speeches, I recount a true incident about missing a turnoff on the Brooklyn-Queens Expressway in New York. To get my audience involved, I begin, "Let me set the scene. It was a sweltering Friday afternoon in July as I pulled up to the tollbooth of the Manhattan Midtown Tunnel. When I rolled down the window, the sticky heat hit me like a boxing glove. The air stank of melting pavement and exhaust fumes. Horns were honking and drivers yelling. Everyone was impatient to get into the tunnel. Everyone except me.

When you start planning how to tell your story, ask yourself the following questions:

● What did it smell like?_____

● What did it taste like? _____

● What did it feel like?_____

● What did it sound like?_____

● What did it look like?_____

Temperatures and tastes and sounds are great for triggering memories and awakening our senses: "the hot, dusty desert," "the crunchy snow underfoot," "the smell of freshly baked bread," "the church bells chiming up the valley."

Of course, your story has to have a valid point. But if it does, your audience will probably remember it long after they have forgotten your latest marketing survey.

Paint a Picture with Words

Particularly in a multi-lingual world, well-chosen words improve your chances of being listened to and understood. Just because you dish out dry and dreary facts at internal staff meetings does not mean you should subject a conference audience to the same fare. Spice up vocabulary and make it more palatable. To fine-tune your language, choose words which are colorful, concrete and concise.

Use Language that Is Colorful, Concrete and Concise

1. Colorful.
You don't need to be a speech writer or have a graduate degree in literature to brighten up your vocabulary. Just read and listen more attentively.

Make an appeal to the ear. Instead of "The office is full of activity." say "The office is humming, buzzing, pulsating, exploding with activity." (Choose just one, of course.)

2. Concrete.

When you listen to someone speak, your brain is capable of assimilating several hundred words a minute. Since most people speak between 140 and 160 words a minute, you have sufficient brain time to analyze, question and contradict what is being said. When your brain is not fully occupied, you may get bored and start daydreaming. This happens with amazing frequency in business speeches. One major reason is that business speakers do not use words which sufficiently engage their listeners.

Here are two abstract examples which metamorphose into concrete images:

❧ A while back > A couple of years ago > In June of 1995, we decided to expand overseas > in Africa > in Kenya and Chad.

❧ Red wine > Australian red wines > 1991 Chauffe Eau Merlot.

3. Concise.

Vague: We invest in training our staff.

Still vague: Recently, we have invested a lot of money in training our sales staff.

Too precise: Within the last 167 days, we have invested $567,213 in training our sales staff.

Just right: Within the last six months, we have invested close to $600,000 in training our sales staff.

In describing his contribution to the field of immunology, Nobel Prize winner Dr. Rolf Zinkernagel said, "This knowledge is as important for immunology as the colors red and green are for drivers."

Include Repetition and Rhyme

1. Repetition.

"The cost was zero!" In her speech a French sales representative described three ways she single-handedly got positive publicity for her product, including an interview on prime time French television. At the end of each example, she paused, looked at her audience and said in her charming accent, "The cost was zero." The following year, I witnessed the lasting impact that the repetition of a good take-home message can have as delegates greeted Silvie with the words, "I remember your talk . . . zee cost was zero."

Repeat the same words at the beginning of two or more sentences:

Let us stand together for . . .
Let us work together . . .
Let us succeed together . . .

2. Rhyme.

It is not a question of composing a sonnet, but if a rhyming couplet walks across your path, grab it. It is easy on the ear and perforates our memories, too. "Stride and glide" is my own creation. It is short, sweet and memorable.

Other rhetorical devices are in short supply in the international business arena nowadays. Expressions like "rhetoric" and "oratory" have a pejorative meaning. In an attempt to be business-like, we have lost a lot of what makes language good to listen to. I encourage my clients not to shy away from expressions that "roll off the tongue" and "sound good to the ear."

Jokes Versus Humor

Do you know what they call someone who speaks three languages? Trilingual. Someone who speaks two languages? Bilingual. And someone who speaks one language? American.

That joke is almost as old as the one where one man says, "I don't have to run faster than the bear, I just have to run faster than you." When you include a joke in your speech, you cannot know in advance whether or not your audience has heard it before. With the advent of joke pages on the Internet, your funny story may arrive at your destination before you do. Besides which, your audience may feel manipulated. They expect more originality from their speakers. They would also prefer something that pertains to your subject and isn't just tacked on for the laugh value. That's why I always suggest that speakers use "home grown" humor, but I realize that my admonitions will not always be heeded, so here is some advice on getting a laugh for your joke.

Approach jokes gently.

If you decide to include a joke, approach it gently. If you say, "Here's a great story I heard last week at the club," you are setting yourself up for failure if your audience doesn't concur. When a joke falls flat among friends, everyone groans and someone jumps in to help you out. In front of two hundred people, no one will come to your rescue.

Weaving a joke into your speech may catch the audience off-guard which can be great fun if they aren't totally nonplussed that you are plying them with humor.

When you get to the end of your joke, take a long pause and deliver the final words with punch! (That is why it's called a punch line.) If your audience refrains from uproarious fits of laughter, shrug your shoulders, smile and continue. If they do laugh, don't interrupt them. Enjoy it. Once the laughter starts to fade, you can resume speaking. As many a stand-up comedian will tell you, the timing is crucial.

Add a touch of humor.
When I talk about humor, I don't mean a joke which has the audience rolling on the floor. I am referring more to a mood, an essence, an approach which says to your audience, "I know we live in difficult times, but we can make life a little more livable if we lighten up."

Here is a story which almost did not reach the audience. At our first coaching session, Mr. Bogdan Banaszczyk, General Director of HCI Poland, told me he would not include an anecdote because so many Americans tell story after story without ever making a point. (I have heard this comment before.) I countered by saying that just because some speakers tell too many stories is no reason not to include a story that does have a message.

At his conference, Mr. Banaszczyk did include a story:

Getting started in Warsaw wasn't easy! For our first delivery to the Marriott Hotel, we were all on hand, but the van failed to arrive.

Suddenly a rusty old Russian van careened around the corner and crashed over the curb of the main entrance. The uniformed doormen in their tufted hats started talking excitedly on their walkie-talkies while the elegant guests stared in amazement. After a huge commotion, the van, belching smoke, skidded down the ramp and almost collided with the luxury automobiles parked there.

It was another two years before Marriott gave us another order.

The audience loved Mr. Banaszyczk's story, which was particularly apt because the conference was at the Marriott Hotel. At the coffee break, one potential customer asked what was in the truck. (Salt tablets for the indoor swimming pool.) Someone else asked about HCI's current relationship with the Marriott Hotel (excellent).

If you get the right flavor and the correct proportion, humor is a wonderful ingredient in a business presentation. Used with a delicate touch, humor can relax, create rapport, make a point, change the mood and occasionally save the day.

> At a Finance Summit, the Polish Minister of Foreign Affairs said, "We didn't always get along with Russia." Suddenly a power failure plunged the conference room into total darkness. With 200 delegates sitting in stunned silence, Darius Rosati continued, "Does that mean I can't talk about Russia? I thought those times were over." The lights flickered on, and the audience applauded Mr. Rosati's quick-witted comments.

If you think to yourself, "I could never come up with a clever comment at short notice," then you probably never will. A negative attitude rarely harvests humor. Words will fail you. Or more correctly, you will fail the words. On the other hand, if you give yourself permission to live in the moment and to trust your intuition, you may be surprised at your ingenuity under duress. The comment that pops out of your mouth has a good chance of being amusing because humor is one way we humans cope with disconcerting and unforeseen events.

On the other hand, humor can be a dangerous weapon if it is misused, either on purpose or unintentionally. Unless you know your audience intimately, avoid sarcasm and biting wit.

In all cases, never tell jokes or make comments with cultural, sexual or racial slurs. Period. That is at the same low level as using profanity in a speech. It is an insult to your audience.

Profiling yourself differently from the other speakers at your conference and including a personal touch will pay off grandly. After all, preparing and practicing a speech is time and energy consuming, and that is only the beginning. Once your speech is ready, you cannot hand it over to DHL. You have to deliver it yourself.

Since you go to all this effort, you want to be remembered, don't you?

CHAPTER

5

Adapt to Make a Connection

"To win this project, we have to make our presence felt in a pregnant way." The startled faces of 30 engineers let the speaker know she had chosen the wrong English equivalent for the German prägnant, which means "succinct." ABB project leader Christine Lange smiled and said, "I do not let a vocabulary mistake worry me as long as I know I am getting my message across."

Christine has the right attitude, and watching her in action, it is obvious that she connects with her audience. As anyone who works in more than one language knows, you are bound to make mistakes from time to time. Although these slips of the tongue may be embarrassing, they are usually harmless. What is important is your attitude and commitment. If your audience senses that you are trying to make a connection, communication can blossom despite vocabulary blunders or grammatical errors.

To connect with your audience, first, you need to get their attention. Crucial in any presentation, it is doubly important that an international audience knows listening to you will be worth the added effort. Second, you need to adapt yourself while maintaining your individuality. Third, you need to present your message clearly and with conviction.

As the speaker, you have to be prepared to meet your audience more than half way. To help you remember, visualize a large "gap" stretching between you and your audience. In order to bridge the gap, you have to:

Get the audience's attention.
Adapt yourself.
Present your message clearly and with conviction.

Get Your Audience's Attention

I used to say that "g stands for grab," but over the years I have realized that "grab" is too American for most of the world. So now I say "get the attention." It sounds better. You see, I have adapted.

One way to get an international audience's attention is by beginning in their language, especially if they are not expecting it!

> A telecommunications expert was invited to deliver the luncheon speech at an official banquet in Lyons. He was told that he could speak in either French or English. He began, *"Mesdames et messieurs, en préparant mon discours pour aujourd'hui, c'était necessaire de prendre une décision très importante: parler à vous en français pour 45 minutes ou prendre 15 minutes pour le même discours en anglais."* He paused. He smiled broadly. And then he said in English, "I hope you agree with my decision." They agreed.

Good work! This speaker captured his audience's attention by making an effort to speak the language of the host country. In his elementary French, he explained that he would need 45 minutes to relay the same message that would take only 15 minutes in English. His audience was readily persuaded, and his self-confession evinced a chuckle which relaxed everyone. Finally, he only spoke for 15 minutes.

Begin in the Language of the Country

Why not begin your talk by greeting your audience in their language? Check in the Country Profiles to read how to say, "Good morning, ladies and gentlemen" (and "Good afternoon, ladies and gentlemen"). You will probably need help with the pronunciation. If you show the appropriate page to a native speaker and explain what you want to do I guarantee you will get the assistance you need. People are eager to help when they see you are taking an interest in them and their language.

Yes, it takes courage. Yes, you may mispronounce a word. But if you consider the first ten seconds as your "verbal handshake" with the audience, it is a great way to get their attention and make a connection.

What do you say after you have said "Hello"? Why not consider telling your audience you are pleased to be with them (and that you know you are in Budapest not Brussels). In some countries, like South Korea, you need to take a diametrically different approach and thank your audience for honoring you with their presence. An appropriate sentence awaits you in each Country Profile. Again, you will want to check out the pronunciation with someone on the spot. Even with a little coaching, you will not sound like a native speaker, but most audiences will give you an enormous amount of credit for trying to speak to them in their language. Particularly for those of us fortunate to have English as our mother tongue, it is a nice way to let an audience know that we do not take this advantage for granted. (And it is an advantage in today's global business world where the lingua franca is currently English.)

Pay Attention to Protocol

In some cultures, speakers are required to begin in a formal manner by addressing the dignitaries by name. Check in the Country Profiles to see what is customary. Then double-check with your hosts.

If you are expected to give a formal introduction, follow the custom carefully. Write the names and titles clearly on a card, spelling phonetically and marking the stressed syllable. (Do not use a scrap of paper. This is not the place for a casual touch.) Beforehand ask someone to help you with the pronunciation and practice the names out loud. You may be tempted to think of these greetings as a "mere formality." However the world has revolved for centuries on protocol. If you are a little too formal at the beginning, you can always loosen up and continue more informally. The reverse is not possible.

Now you are ready to bridge to the introduction to your speech. You will find great ways to begin your presentation in Chapter 3. You may already be itching to tell your audience about your great business plan, but it may be wiser not to move too quickly. Americans are eager to "get down to business," but much of the rest of the world takes a little longer. As the saying goes, "Before I care how much you know, I want to know how much you care." Cringe if you will, but as with all clichés, there is a kernel of truth in the core.

When you are speaking in an international situation, you will probably need to adapt yourself if you want to make a positive connection.

Adapt Your Verbal Delivery

No matter what language you are speaking, the following suggestions will get you started:

🕭 Slow down 10 percent at the beginning.

🕭 Articulate words carefully.

🕭 Pace yourself by watching the audience.

🕭 Pause.

🕭 Repeat a sentence occasionally. Repeat a sentence occasionally.

For more specifics about delivery, please refer to Chapter 7.

Adapt Your English for Non-Native English Speaking Audiences

One of the main stumbling blocks when you are giving a formal speech is that you are doing all the talking. Unless you are in an informal atmosphere, no one will raise a hand and ask you to repeat or explain what you have said. Audience members do not want to admit confusion, especially in a language which they have supposedly mastered.

That is why you need to watch your audience carefully to see whether they are with you. You have to listen with your eyes. If everyone is leaning forward, nodding emphatically, and taking notes, you can be fairly sure they are following what you are saying.

What, however, if everyone closes their eyes and seems to be nodding off. What does that signal? It depends upon the culture. Your audience may be listening intently and absorbing every nuance of your speech. Some cultures produce excellent listeners who are trained to retain spoken language. On the other hand, they may actually be nodding off. How can you tell?

First, check the Country Profiles to learn what kind of audience response to expect. If, as you are speaking, you are still uncertain whether or not you are being understood, you can incorporate a long pause. Just stop talking and wait. If you have the courage to endure the "pregnant pause" (as we say in English), you will see the audience's reaction. If they open their eyes questioningly as if to ask, "Why are you pausing?" you can continue at ease. If they look as if they have just been jolted back into the conference room, they probably have been.

If you know your audience does not have English as their first language, you need to make some adaptations when you are preparing your speech.

Simplify by using shorter words and sentences. Don't obfuscate your message by showing off your vocabulary. You will confuse your audience.

Explain terms and acronyms the very first time you use them. Say, "We deal in Fast Moving Consumer Goods which we abbreviate as FMCG," or "We're moving into the Maghreb region which is shorthand for the countries, Morocco, Algeria and Tunisia."

At the United Nations Environment Program in Geneva, speakers tossed out acronyms gratuitously. Finally one speaker took the situation in hand in a humorous way. In a charming Scottish brogue, he announced, "My speech will only contain two acronyms: BATNEEC which stands for the Best Available Technology Not Exceeding Excessive Costs and CATNIP which designates the Cheapest Available Technology Not Involving Prostitution." He got a laugh, and the other speakers got the point. From then on, the acronyms were explained. The multi-lingual audience could follow along, and everyone learned a lot more.

Eliminate jargon which is natural to you, but which might bewilder your audience. Americans love baseball terms, but if you say, "All I wanted was a ballpark figure," or "That idea never made it to first base," you may leave your audience out in left field.

Preview and rehearse your speech with someone who understands your audience and can advise you.

Adapt When You Speak in a Second Language

Speaking in a second (or third) language is a challenge. I know because many of my clients do not have English as their mother tongue. One major advantage is that these speakers have to think before they speak. That is inevitably a benefit for all!

Having spoken in German on several occasions, I can vouch for the increased amount of preparation time and stamina which are necessary to be effective when you are speaking in a second language.

When I moderated a banquet in Munich, I wrote out each introduction in faultless German and practiced out loud. So far, so good. But at the actual event, I used my word-for-word script. When I reviewed the videotape later, I saw my mistake. I had spent too much time referring to my script instead of connecting with my audience. I should have used speaker notes. After all, I had been chosen to moderate because of my lively and entertaining manner, not because I speak German perfectly!

If you are speaking in a language other than your mother tongue, forget about perfection. Aim for a connection!

If necessary, write out your speech word for word. Then practice it out loud, but when the time comes, throw away your manuscript and work from speaker notes. When you begin, resist the temptation to say, "I hope you can understand my English," or "Please forgive my school girl French." An audience will happily overlook small blunders and enjoy your "charming accent" if you just get on with your message.

Keep your sentences uncomplicated, and write out the difficult words phonetically: (fo net' i cally). Then of course, you need to practice out loud. You have to be able to get your tongue around those strange sounds. If you tape yourself on a Dictaphone (or with a video camera), you will readily hear (and see) what improvements to make.

Prior to your speaking event, submerge yourself by reading newspapers and listening to radio and TV in the language you will be speaking. Total immersion before speaking can improve your fluency exponentially.

But do not overextend yourself. Your audience will forgive your less-than-perfect French or Spanish, but if you mangle one of their beloved quotations from Baudelaire or Cervantes, they might cringe. Stand up to speak up!

At a large meeting, the speaker read her speech without standing up. Sitting behind a desk lectern, she was invisible to the majority of the audience. When asked why she remained seated, she replied, "My Portuguese isn't perfect. I thought if I didn't stand up no one would notice."

Adapt a Speech that Is Prepared for You by Someone Else

Be sure that the translator uses language and phraseology which is suitable for you.

Don't hide behind the lectern.

As the director of a not-for-profit international organization in Switzerland, Ketty Ronzani, who is from Argentina, was asked to speak to a local club in German. She drafted her remarks in English (which is the official language of her organization) and gave them to the company's translator who produced a sophisticated German text which was far too complicated for her. After she took one look at his convoluted language, she crossed out every word she could not pronounce easily. Then she asked him for a simpler version which she practiced out loud several times. Fortified with newfound confidence and courage, Ketty threw away her word-for-word manuscript and used speaker notes on the actual day. At her conclusion, she received rousing applause and several invitations to deliver her speech to other clubs. How's that for knowing you have succeeded!

Get Your Audience Involved

If your mind goes blank (this can happen in your native language, too), look at the audience hopefully. Smile. Chances are that someone will supply the word. This assumes, of course, that your message has kept your audience hanging on every word.

When Dr. Harry Verschuuren, a Dutch toxicologist, arrived to deliver a presentation, the organizers asked him to speak in French. Although Dr. Verschuuren speaks French (as well as Dutch, German and English), he had planned to speak in English, but being an accommodating man, he acquiesced. During his speech, he paused to search for a word en français. Suddenly someone from the audience called it out. From then on, whenever he hesitated, someone came to his rescue. Afterwards, the participants agreed his speech was the best at the entire conference, and they had enjoyed being actively involved!

Let Your Interpreter Help You

Interpreters are your lifeline to your audience, not (as some speakers seem to think) another piece of equipment which switches on and off automatically. Avoid using "interpreter" and "translator" interchangeably. The difference is basic. Translation deals with the written word; interpretation is an oral process. Interpreters will be pleased if you know the difference. They will also appreciate your providing the following before you arrive:

Text of your speech or your speaker notes. You may be asked to submit a complete manuscript. Do not hesitate to turn in a "written text" and then speak from notes. In fact, good interpreters prefer someone who speaks freely. Your natural pauses give them time to "catch up." When you read a speech word-for-word, your voice becomes dull and lifeless and makes their job harder.

Vocabulary list: Most interpreters are aware that an NGO is a non-government organization but may not know the difference between an enneagram and an angiogram.

Magazine article about your subject.

Text or synopsis of video or audio tapes you will be using.

Please find your way to the interpreters' booths and introduce yourself beforehand. Assuming that you have sent materials ahead, this is the time to ask the interpreters if they have any questions. The better prepared they are, the better they will get your message across for you. They will appreciate your thoughtfulness. Remember, you need them to make a connection.

Simultaneous Interpretation

This type of interpretation is used at large conferences. Audience members wear headphones, and the speaker is interpreted simultaneously, perhaps into several languages. Since the interpreters work within soundproof booths, they only hear what is transmitted through the sound system. That means you should only speak when your voice is being amplified.

If you can see the interpreters from where you are standing, an occasional glance during your presentation will ascertain that all is going smoothly.

> When Dr. Roy Quartermaine spoke in Brazil, he supplied the interpreter with a list of terms, including "propylene glycol monomethyl ether," which is the reverse order in Portuguese: "monomethyl ether of glycol propylene." The interpreter suggested he pause briefly before using it to give her a head start. Since he could see her in the booth, he paused, she started and gave him a nod to continue. The system worked like a charm. Just before he concluded, he gestured to the booth and thanked her.

Why not take a tip from experienced speakers who acknowledge the interpreters at some point in their speeches. It shows you are comfortable and in control.

If you take a question from someone in the audience who is not using a microphone, repeat it so the interpreter can hear and translate it. Remember that your interpreters are "caged" in soundproof booths. They can only hear via microphones. Even handing an audience member a microphone is no guarantee that it will be used correctly. I have seen questioners hold the microphone at arm's length and gesture with it. Although it is the conference moderator's job to step in and say something, it's your presentation that loses momentum, so why not take the initiative and say, "Please speak directly into the microphone so the interpreters can hear you."

Do not be surprised if your audience reacts only after a delay of a few seconds. It often takes time for your words to be translated.

> Dr. Daniela Ball spoke in Kobe, Japan to three hundred businessmen and researchers at a symposium sponsored by the Organization of Coffee Companies. At the end of her 30-minute presentation, nothing happened. Not knowing what to do, she stood silently for what seemed an eternity. Finally after 30 seconds (which is an eternity when you do not know what is happening), her audience began applauding. Obviously it had taken the interpreter that long to conclude.

Consecutive Interpretation

Consecutive interpretation is usually used in one-to-one and more informal speaking situations. The speaker utters one or two sentences and then pauses to allow the interpreter to speak.

> For each of Whirlpool's five trade fairs throughout China, Roy Armes, president and managing director of Whirlpool China, ensured faultless presentations by engaging a top notch interpreter with whom he worked in advance. They devised a practical setup whereby he stood alone on the stage and she sat at a table in the first row facing him. He formally introduced the interpreter who stood briefly to let everyone know whose voice they would be hearing. This arrangement allowed Mr. Armes and the interpreter to have close eye contact with each other. She could adapt to his pace. He could check to see that things were moving along smoothly.

Making sure that your message is getting across to your audience the way you want it to is crucial for the success of your presentation. Sometimes, interpreters try to steal the show:

> An economist (fluent in both English and French) was asked to speak to a bilingual audience. To avoid delivering in both languages, he spoke in English while a French interpreter stood next to him. Every two sentences he paused to allow her to relay his ideas in French. Suddenly he stopped, turned to her and said, "Please do not add your editorial comments."

To ascertain that interpreters are getting your message across and not theirs, check out credentials. If need be, have someone in the audience monitor and signal if the interpretation is inaccurate or misleading.

Adapt Your Non-Verbal Delivery

In daily life, your face and body are constantly expressing your feelings, your reactions, your moods. A lifted eyebrow queries a coworker's comment, your fingertips tapping on a table telegraph impatience, a broad smile reflects a good news message.

Check out your interpreter's credentials in advance.

When business people walk around wearing a mask of calculated blandness, it is usually to conceal their ignorance of supply-side economics, the capital of Pakistan or how to use the espresso machine.

If everyone sitting around the conference table has the same frame of reference, a deadpan face and expressionless voice will not obliterate the speaker's ideas. There may be boredom in the boardroom, but the message will get through.

However, as soon as more than one culture or language is present, communication becomes more complex. You can help your audience understand you by underlining and emphasizing your message with expansive gestures and animated facial expression. Let your eyes blaze with excitement about the latest sales figures. Move with urgency to the flip chart when explaining the joint venture. Let your hands trace an arc to show your global expansion into other markets.

The chances that you will exaggerate are minimal. The chances are much greater that you will clam up and do nothing. It happens all the time. As soon as most people stand in front of an audience they become stiff and unnatural. They stick their hands in their pockets or behind their backs. Better yet, they barricade themselves behind the lectern. And the lecterns are usually huge.

Especially when you and your audience do not share the same mother tongue, you need to optimize the visual cues in your presentation. Bold and

graphic visual aids will make your message more accessible to your audience. Read more in Chapter 6. But as it says there, you are your best visual
aid. Use your hands! You may feel awkward using your hands more than
you normally do. However, unhabitual behavior is not necessarily unnatural. You may have just forgotten how to move naturally and with purpose.

Consider a practice session to polish your gestures. After all, if you want
to improve your golf stance or your backhand, you invest time and energy
and probably hire a coach who corrects your weak points and encourages
you to improve.

Gesture at waist level and above.

Gestures can open doors for you, especially when words do not suffice.
However, inappropriate language and gestures might shut some doors right
in your face. In North America, there is an expressive hand gesture that uses
the thumb and first finger to signify success. It is a very positive "A-OK!" In
South America and Europe, this gesture has an altogether different meaning
which is not used in polite company. If you are traveling to a foreign country, it pays to be prepared. In addition to checking out the Country Profiles,
check online for international business etiquette. Then once you have
arrived, stop talking and start observing closely.

Now you are two-thirds across the GAP. You know how to grab, whoops, get your audience's attention, and you are prepared to adapt to make a connection. Now all you have to do is present your message clearly and with conviction. You will find suggestions throughout *Speaking Globally*.

Use Visuals that Work

The lights dim as the next speaker approaches the front of the room. Before you even have a chance to look at her, the first slide appears with her name and title. The second slide announces her talk. The third slide gives an overview. Slide follows slide, bombarding you with illegible words and numbers while somewhere in the darkness a disembodied voice drones on. Thirty minutes later, you hear the magic words, "Last slide, please."

Unless you have just joined the business world, you have probably witnessed such a presentation. In fact, you may have even given one. The above description is a reminder that visual aids cannot take your place. They cannot tell your story. Only you can do that. What visual aids can do is serve as a powerful tool.

Especially necessary in a multi-lingual situation, you need to optimize the visual! The cards in airlines explain emergency procedures in pictures, and they are understood by everyone.

If you need slides, make sure they support your message, not dominate it. Be forewarned that the number of slides you show is in inverse proportion to the effectiveness of your presentation. Whenever possible, I counsel my clients to speak without any slides at all.

If you succumb to slides, limit yourself. The old rule is "one slide, one message, one minute." Here's my updated version: You speak for one minute (the audience needs to get used to you before you introduce another element). Then you show 2–10 slides in 2 minutes. Then you insert a blank slide and talk to your audience again without any distractions. Then another cluster of slides. And so on. Make sure that your final slide displays your take-home message boldly. If it stays on during your Q&A session or even into the coffee break, it is a visual reminder of your talk. Much better than the "Thank you for your attention" slide that usually appears.

Guidelines for Great Graphics

Here are suggestions for making PowerPoint slides or transparencies for the overhead projector. By the way, although a "slide" is always called a "slide," many names exist for transparencies, including acetates, overheads, flimsies, folios and sometimes even slides.

1. Use Landscape Format   not   Portrait Format

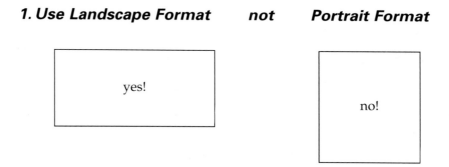

Screens were designed for film and are universally wider than they are high, so use them this way to get optimal value.

2. Creating Templates

Set up your template before you start. Choose a simple template. Complicated backgrounds detract from the message itself. Use the master slide view and set up all text boxes, typefaces, logos and any design elements that will be on every slide on this master to give your presentation a consistent look. (If copying slides from several presentations, set up the new template first. Then copy/paste old slides into the template, not vice versa.)

3. Title Boxes

Put the message in the title box, not the name of your company or "Financial Forecast." Every title box needs a different message. Short and relevant. This forces you to figure out what you are saying and lets your audience know instantly. Use the title/body text boxes as you have set up on the master slide. Moving them will result in a different look on each slide. Your audience will notice the movement as you advance from slide to slide.

4. Colors

The background should be dark. Some speakers say, "I use normal slides instead of those trendy ones with dark backgrounds." What they do not realize is that dark backgrounds are easier on your audience's eyes. Eyes get tired of looking at white backgrounds. It's like looking at a blank screen. When do we use glaring, bright lights? To intimidate people in criminal interrogations. Not the mood you want to establish. The print should be yellow or white.

5. Font Style

Choose Helvetica, Arial or another sans serif bold print which is easier to read on a screen, particularly from a distance or if the equipment is slightly out of focus. "Sans serif" does not have the little feet which connect one letter to another the way a serif font does. Those connections make it easier to read books or newspaper, but not words on a screen. This is a serif font again. It was developed for use in newspapers.
Use a "natural mix" of upper and lower case letters. DON'T USE JUST CAPITAL LETTERS, EXCEPT FOR HEADLINES. THEY ARE HARD TO READ. *Do not use italics; they are also difficult to read.*

6. Choose 24 to 32 pt. Font Size

You want the guy in the very back row to see too, right? Audiences do not like to hear the question, "Can you see this in the back?" because the answer to that question is always, "No!" Audiences resent being told that "I know you cannot see this slide, but I want to discuss it anyway."

7. Charts

Charts lend themselves well to the slide format, especially when the point they make is evident.

Bar charts: Don't use the 3D effect. Don't use thin lines or markers on the lines. When you compare, put contrasting colors side by side (orange next to green, not orange next to red.)

Pie charts: Use maximum of 5-6 pieces of pie. Put labels on the slices, not outside the pie.

Spider charts: Use no more than three data sets.

Don't group too many similar charts together (Instead show a bar chart, then a pie chart, then a spider chart, then bar chart, pie chart, spider chart . . . are you getting tired? So is your audience.)

8. Use Pictures and Symbols

Audiences respond positively to symbols and pictures. It's not surprising, is it? Most of us remember faces, but forget names. We recall entire scenes from films but are hard pressed to repeat the accompanying dialogue. We dream in pictures, not words. When we are trying to get our bearings, we recall buildings and landmarks better than street names and numbers. In my workshops, I insist that participants create visuals using no words at all. The results are creative and powerful. Having said this, I recommend you include clip art sparingly. We have all seen the gypsy fortune-teller and the detective! Also be aware that cartoons (like Dilbert), photographs and other images may be copyrighted and should only be used with permission.

9. Word Slides

Think of a six-pack (of cola or beer). Maximum six lines, six words per line. Better yet, think three-pack. Use verbs and be sure they are similar. For example, To speak successfully you need to

- prepare
- practice
- present (better than "preparation, to practice and presenting"}

How to Operate the Equipment

Find out in advance how to operate the equipment. In your dry-run, use the very same laptop you will use for the actual presentation. Be sure to bring an adaptor. Even within countries sockets may be different. Check that the colors and typefaces look the same on the big screen as they did in your office. Check also that your slides are legible. If you are using a remote control, find out where you have to aim it to advance the slides.

If a technician will handle your presentation, mutually figure out how you will cue him to advance your slides.

When a slide comes on the screen, pause two seconds until the audience has a chance to focus on it. Then begin talking about it. Look at the audience. Do not keep your eyes glued to the screen. You may take a quick peek to be sure you are talking about the right slide, but that's all!

If you need to use a pointer, there's too much on your slide. However, if you do use a laser pointer, do not inscribe arabesques on the screen. Point with a steady hand. If you are shaking, the pointer will shake, too. Better yet, tell your audience where to look with words. You can say, "If you look at the left column" or "the yellow piece of the pie." Or you could have drawn a circle/box around the special information when you were making your slides.

How to Use the OHP

Locate the on/off button or panel. It's at a different place on every model. Practice focusing and adjusting the height of the lens so everyone in the audience can see the transparencies. If there isn't a spare bulb built into the base, locate one beforehand. If you intend to use pens, bring your own. Be sure they are thick and intended for use on transparencies. Bring some empty transparencies, just in case. Check that there is sufficient roll-through paper, if you plan to use it.

Do not use your finger or a pen to point. Use words to point: "Please look at the center column." Turn off when not in use. The OHP was developed to use without turning your back to your audience. The lights can stay on.

Using Videotapes

When they are well-made, videotapes are a powerful and dramatic means of presenting materials, showing action scenes and production processes. If, however, you have a 30-minute video clip of soil degradation in Ethiopia, you probably need only to show the 60 relevant seconds. Preset the video to the right place. Then tell your story and start the video just before the high point.

If you want to include a videotape, double check that it is the right format and system for the conference center. Every time a video is copied, it loses 12 percent resolution, so use an original not a copy.

If you will be showing a videotape, the playback equipment must be compatible.

Nowadays, most hotels and conference centers in Asia and Europe are equipped with multi-system video playback equipment. However, if you neglect to check it out in advance, you will discover your conference center is the exception. (In North America, the multi-system is not as widely used, so you may be limited to showing NTSC formatted videos).

TV Norms:

❂ NTSC (National Television Standard Committee): Used in USA, Canada, Mexico, South Korea, Philippines, Taiwan, Japan, Chile.

❂ PAL (Phase Alternating Line): Used in Europe, excluding France.

❂ Secam (Sequentielle Couleur à Mémoire): Used in France, Albania, Bulgaria, Cyprus, Greece, Poland, Romania, Czech Republic, Hungary.

Monitors:
RGB (Red Green Blue) monitors project "video beams" onto a large screen and are well suited to large audiences. When a RGB system is unavailable, several monitors can be installed along the sides of the room. Remember if your audience has difficulty seeing your video, they will blame you.

Flip Chart

If your audience is not larger than 50, make friends with a flip chart. It's user-friendly, has many advantages over more sophisticated equipment and does not need to be plugged in. Do, however, check that you have enough paper and thick pens.

Whenever possible, use pictures rather than words. Yes, I know you are not an artist, but even the simplest of pictures will capture the audience's attention, stick figures, for example. Draw quickly and simply. The technique requires minimal practice and a little daring. Since you will be

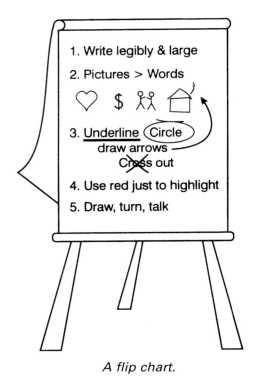

A flip chart.

explaining at the same time, you have a lot of leeway. (If someone walks into the room after your speech and cannot decipher what you have drawn, never mind. The flip chart is for instantaneous recognition.)

Occasionally speakers prepare their flip charts in advance. This can give you a sense of security, but it reduces the immediacy of watching you create on the spot.

Handouts

Handouts are a great way to make sure your message gets taken home if you keep them concise. The fewer pages you produce, the greater chance your material will be looked at again.

Hanneke C. Frese, Head of Group Capabilities of Zurich Financial Services, knows that conference participants get overloaded with printouts of PowerPoint slides. For her talk to international HR managers, she created a little laminated card as her only handout. One side said, "You have the

Give out the handouts afterwards.

right to remain undisturbed." At the bottom were the words "a portable, little idea" and her name. The other side listed her seven points for retaining and motivating talented employees. Two weeks later, when Hanneke observed a colleague showing the card to another employee, she knew her idea was a hit. Now whenever she speaks, Hanneke produces a "portable, little idea."

To distribute or not to distribute? Generally, it is better to hand out your material after you speak. Otherwise you may discover that instead of listening, your audience is reading the hard copies and getting ahead of you. Be sure that your name, your firm's name, phone and fax are on your take-home materials.

Models and Objects

As long as your model or map illustrates your message and is large enough to be seen by everyone in your audience, use it!

Speaking in Kansas City, Missouri, I tacked up a world map and indicated, "Look! Here we are right in the middle of the United States. And according to this map, the United States is the center of the world. But the world is round." Then I pulled out a large inflated beach ball globe and continued, "Kansas City is not always in the center of the world, and we have to remember that when we are discussing Global Communication Programs."

At the same conference, another speaker wore a pair of gigantic sunglasses to illustrate her organization's bright future. Her cute gag backfired because she kept the glasses on. Nobody could see her eyes.

If you want to read a passage from a book, here's a useful trick. Type the passage in a large size font and then secure the paper in the book with tape or paper clips. You will be able to show the book and read the passage without resorting to putting on your glasses.

If you are showing a bottle of your latest sugar-free soft drink in your presentation, keep it out of sight until you refer to it. (Stash it in the lectern or at the side of the stage.) Then, when you are finished with it, put it aside.

Demonstrations

A fitting and well-executed demonstration is a great way to engage your audience because it contains the elements of "lights, sound, action!"

A California fitness expert spoke to senior executives who were interested in establishing a health program for their employees. First, she wrote the word "heart" on the flip chart. Later she drew a diagram of a heart. Finally she reached into her briefcase, pulled out a jump rope and skipped while making her final plea for exercise: "A hundred skips a day keeps a heart attack away." Exaggerated, you may think, but in Amsterdam, they loved her energy and awarded her the contract. She had escalated her supporting materials with great success. Starting with written words, she proceeded to a picture of a heart, and finally using a day-glo yellow skipping rope, she demonstrated being in good shape herself.

You are your best visual aid.

You Are Your Best Visual Aid

It was the end of a long day. The White House Commission on Alternative Medicine had heard 80 petitions by the time Barbara Sarah took the stage. All day she had worn a jaunty cap with "Celebrate Life" on the front. While speaking, she kept the cap on. A bit unusual for a woman in her fifties, but she wanted her message to be unforgettable. She said to the weary committee, "I am talking to you today wearing three hats, so to speak. I work in Oncology at the national level." Then she removed the baseball cap and continued, "I work in Oncology for my local community." She reached up and slowly removed her auburn

FIGURE 6.1 The typeface is size 28 Univers Bold. If you choose a smaller size, you will have to ask, "Can you see this in the back?" and you know the answer, don't you? Cut out the visual clutter and create slides that are clear and simple.

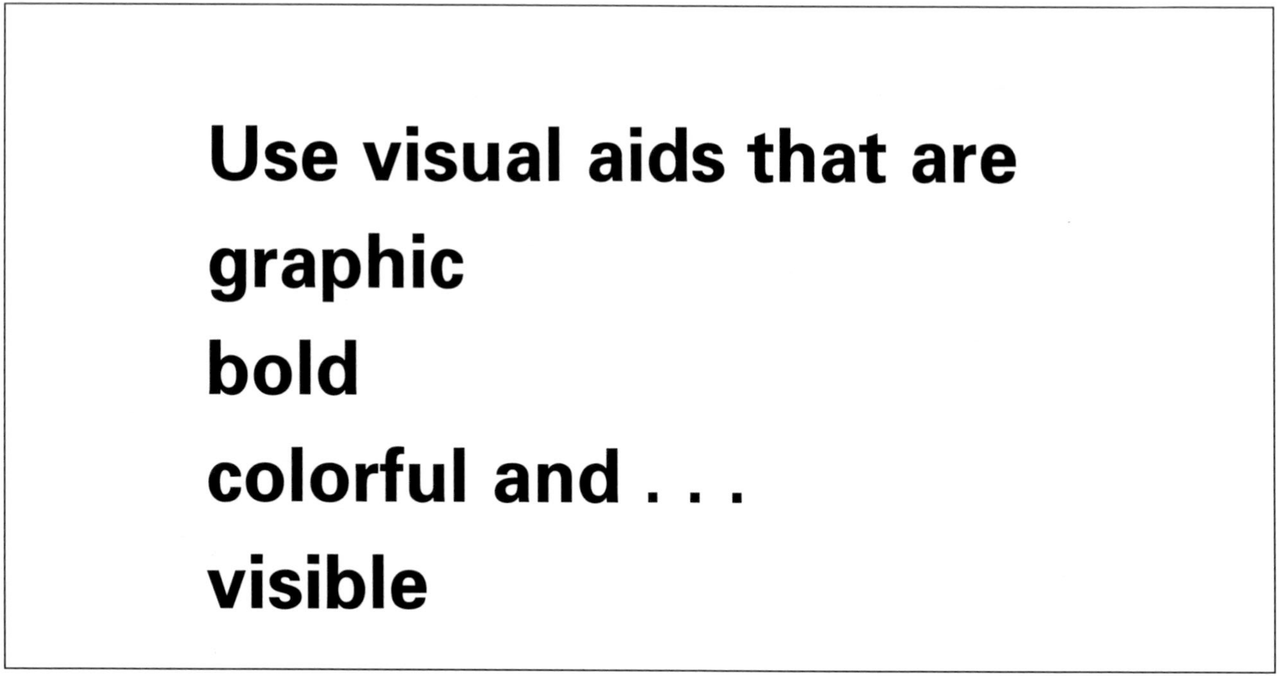

Use visual aids that are

graphic

bold

colorful and . . .

visible

hair, startling her audience into rapt attention. She stood with a base-ball cap in one hand and a wig in the other. On her head? Short gray curls. "I am here on a personal level, too. I am a cancer survivor, and my hair did grow back. We need more research in the field of alternative medicine."

Did the Commission take note of Barbara Sarah and her message? Yes, indeed. Proof that you can be your best visual aid.

7

Deliver Your Message with Power and Comfort

An energetic woman strides to the front of the room, springs up the two steps and crosses to the center of the stage. She glances pleasantly at the audience as she places her first transparency on the overhead projector. Then she turns to face the audience and plants both feet firmly on the floor. She looks at two people in the audience and waits until they return her gaze. Her face seems to say, "It's good to be here with you today. I have some amazing news!" Then and only then does she begin speaking.

Another speaker shuffles to the front, mounts the steps and turns on the overhead projector. With his back to the audience, he starts talking to the chart on the screen.

Which speaker makes a better first impression? Which speaker are you? Remember, you never have a second chance to make a first impression, and like it or not, first impressions are particularly important when you are speaking at an international conference.

Before you read any farther, please note that if your message is crucially important, you can speak standing on your head, and the audience will give you their undivided attention. If you are explaining how to evacuate a burning building (the one you are in), your voice will convey a sense of urgency. Your body language will be strong and expressive. These are the characteristics of a good delivery. The challenge is to incorporate them into speaking situations when not dealing with life and death issues.

This chapter is divided into four sections:

❧ The Stride and Glide Technique

❧ 3-B Exercises for Controlling Nerves

❧ Positive Body Language

❧ Voice Power

The Stride and Glide Technique

Putting The Stride and Glide Technique to work when you speak will multiply your chances for success! What follows is a 1045 word description which takes several minutes to read but less than thirty seconds to execute. Once you have practiced it, the take-off and landing of your presentation will be a lot smoother. (I usually give my clients options, but I consider The Stride and Glide Technique obligatory.)

Stride

Stride with ease and conviction to the front of the room. (To be explicit, "striding" is walking with purpose.)

If you are carrying a manuscript or folios, smile briefly to the audience to indicate, "I will be with you as soon as things are fully organized." Then proceed to get operational.

Attach the microphone.

Resist putting your wristwatch on the lectern. (Speakers who do that never stick to their time limits.)

Turn and face your audience fully. Try not to stand behind the lectern. The audience needs to see you from head to toe.

Ground yourself. Both feet should be parallel and pointed forward, six to eight inches apart. Distribute your weight evenly on both feet. Imagine that the heels of your feet are growing roots right into the floor. From the waist down, you should be as solid as an oak tree.

Place your hands in the "ready position" — at waist level and ready to gesture. You may lightly clasp them with your palms facing upwards. (Resist holding on to a chair, the lectern or your other hand.)

Alternative position: Let your arms hang at your sides. Although this looks natural, it may feel awkward at first. Since your audience interprets the slightest twitching in your fingers as a sign of nervousness, your hands and fingers must be relaxed. Practice letting your arms hang and your

Two starting positions.

hands dangle. The drawback of this "starting position" is that you have to raise your hands quite a distance when you want to gesture. You may be tempted not to gesture. Before long you will look like a wooden soldier. When you realize that, you will begin to look like a nervous wooden soldier. (Later in this chapter gesturing will be dealt with more fully.)

Keep your hands out where we can see them. Avoid the executive "fig leaf" or the "executive hostage." You may think hands in your pockets convey an insouciant style, but you are really signaling insecurity. Don't take my word for this. Start your own independent research study. Notice when people put their hands in their pockets. It is when they are ill at ease or confronted with a strange or uncomfortable situation. Crossing your arms is very defensive.

Resist fiddling with your hair or touching any part of your body. These mannerisms are magnified when you are in front of an audience. The message they transmit is not positive.

Establish eye contact. Look at one person in the audience. Your look will almost always be returned with a smile or at least a brief encouraging glance. Then look at someone else and repeat the process. This alerts everyone that you are ready to begin and that you want to connect with them. If you have always avoided the audience by gazing six inches above their

The executive line-up.

heads, you have been missing an opportunity to establish rapport with an entire group of human beings, most of whom are hoping that you will succeed. In certain cultures, such as Japan, direct eye contact in one-to-one situations is not acceptable, but when you are delivering a speech, you need to look at your audience.

The initial expression on your face should say, "I am glad to be here. I have a good message, and I am sure you will appreciate it." Let your face light up like it does when you unexpectedly meet a good friend or see a puppy frisking in the park. Do not confuse this with an artificial toothpaste commercial grin. This look needs to be genuine.

Now begin speaking!

Glide

If you receive applause when you finish, acknowledge it with a gracious smile. Don't rush off. Enjoy this well-earned moment. (An audience shows its appreciation by applauding. If you brush it off, you are insulting them.) As the applause subsides, remove the microphone. Give another appreciative look to the audience and glide off until you reach your chair. ("Gliding" has an unstudied grace and elegance, formerly associated with royalty.)

Sit with casual comportment. Let not a grimace darken your visage nor a sigh of relief escape your lips. This is neither the time nor the place to admit to a lapse of memory or a mispronounced word. The audience has probably forgotten, and you cannot do anything about it now anyway. (Take a lesson from the Olympic ice skater who falls executing a triple axel turn. Kerplop! She hits the ice. Without losing a beat, she picks herself up and continues skating with a winning smile on her face.)

Now you have had a step-by-step description of The Stride and Glide Technique. Practice it from start to finish. Stride, ground yourself, get your hands ready, connect with your eyes, let your face glow. Then stop and imagine that you have delivered your entire talk. Hear the applause. Acknowledge it. Glide off. Sit calmly. Flash a regal smile at everyone and hold it until the attention is on the next speaker.

If you are still not convinced about the importance of your beginning and ending, then think about the TV cameras at a marathon or the grand prix. Where do they congregate? At the start and the finish lines.

Once you have mastered The Stride and Glide Technique, you may want to experiment and be the exception that proves the rule. Go ahead! Begin at the rear of the auditorium tossing out questions and humorous remarks as you stride to the lectern. Or begin by pacing back and forth across the stage staring ominously without uttering a word. After all, "All the world's a stage." For most conference presentations, however, The Stride and Glide Technique will serve you well!

Stride and Glide

1. Get ready while seated. Take slow deep breaths. Think positively.

2. *Stride* to the front.

3. Ground yourself with hands in the ready position.

4. Look at two people and wait until they return your look. Create curiosity within the audience.

5. Let your face say: "I have a great message for you!"

6. Begin with a strong voice and gesture with both hands.

7. At the conclusion, let the audience know by slowing down.

8. End with finality and resolution in your voice.

9. Then stand quietly to signal that you have finished.

10. *Glide* back to your seat with a smile on your face.

Control Your Nerves with the 3-B Exercises

An audience cannot feel your clammy hands or hear your pounding heart. Even if they have a slight suspicion that you are suffering from stagefright, they will ignore it if you let them. First, they are grateful that it is you up there, not them. Second, they cannot really help you much except by smiling encouragingly.

That is why you need to make a concerted effort to conceal your anxiety and nervousness by presenting a composed appearance. This is not intended to maliciously deceive an audience. It is to relieve them.

> It is Thomas's first piano recital. He trots up to the piano and scoots onto the piano bench. His feet don't even touch the floor. As he places his hands on the keyboard, everyone in the room audibly inhales. An audience of moms, dads, and relatives holds its collective breath, fervently hoping that Thomas will hit the right notes, and that he won't lose his place and start crying. Just let him get through it, they pray.

Your audience has the same concern. They want you to succeed. Since they are ill-equipped to wipe your sweaty brow or hold your hand, you need to reassure them that "All is well." (The one or two who would like you to fail are the ones who want your job. This is not the time to worry about them.)

The best antidote to sweaty palms and churning stomach is being well prepared and well rehearsed.

If you can convince your audience at the very beginning of your presentation that you are comfortable and in control, they will relax. You will sense a positive feeling emanating from the audience. Then you will be able to relax and enjoy your presentation.

Many speakers take too long to get started. They ramble on and say nothing for 30 seconds. By now the speaker is feeling better about himself and the situation. The audience, however, may be collectively dozing off.

Warm up on your own time! How would you react if a swimmer jumped in the pool and splashed around before his race or the soprano came out on stage and practiced her high notes?

Breathing Time

When the moment arrives for you to be introduced, your heart beats faster, your palms get sweaty and your stomach starts to do somersaults. It's unavoidable. Even professionals experience stage fright before they begin. To quote two great performers:

Helen Hayes, First Lady of American Theater: "Of course, I get butter-flies before I go on stage. But now I have them flying in formation."

Sir Lawrence Olivier: "How do I manage? I walk out on the stage and amaze myself with my own daring."

Dozens of books exist which describe sure-fire ways to relax by reducing nervous tension. Whether geared to corporate go-getters, competitive athletes or expectant mothers, these books all agree that breathing is vitally important. Here is a simple breathing exercise which will help you to relax and focus on the task at hand. It has three good features:

🕭 You can learn it easily.

🕭 You can remember it readily.

🕭 You can do it anywhere.

Begin by exhaling all the air soundlessly out of your lungs through your mouth. Push your diaphragm upwards to expel every last bit. (The diaphragm is a wall of muscle and connective tissue which separates your lungs from your abdominal cavity. If you are not sure where it is, place your hands at about waist level and pant like a dog. What you feel moving in and out is your diaphragm.)

Slowly and regularly inhale through your nose until your lungs are filled to bursting. As you do this, concentrate on your breathing. Avoid distractions.

With your lungs filled to capacity, pause and silently count to three. This interim period between exhalation and inhalation is necessary or you risk hyperventilating.

Exhale, inhale, pause again. Find your own rhythm. Focus solely on your breathing. Repeat at least five times.

Check to see that your tongue is not on the roof of your mouth. It should be resting in the lower part of your mouth cavity in a relaxed position.

Practice this exercise every day. Let it become a handy reflex to the minor inconveniences of civilization. Use it when you are stuck in a traffic jam or when the hotel receptionist cannot find your reservation. And, of course, use it before every presentation you give. You can do this seated in your chair just before you are introduced.

You will have an assuring sense of calmness. You will be more focused on what you are doing.

In addition to calming you down, the other benefit of incorporating deep breathing into your life is to increase your supply of oxygen. Your lungs are incredibly efficient organs. If the lower parts are not used, i.e. filled up regularly, they shut down. A diminished amount of air causes light and shallow breathing. You need a full tank of air to energize your words. You want to end each sentence without fading out because you are running out of breath.

Some of that oxygen gets carried to your brain where it helps you to make quick assessments and adapt your message even as you speak.

When you breathe in and out, concentrate on what you are doing. Take this time to center yourself and be kind to yourself.

Just before you stand up to speak, forgive yourself in advance for any mistake you might make. If you strive to control every contingency, your speech will either be boring or slick. Don't strive to get rid of all the rough edges. Remember, this is a live performance!

Do you resemble a turtle?

Body Work

Do you unconsciously assume an awkward position when you speak? Check out your body. Is your entire upper body tense? Are your shoulders hunched up? Do you resemble a turtle with its head just partially out its shell? Called the "startle reaction," this position is our instinctive reaction to fear. The next time an unexpected loud noise catches you off guard, calibrate how your body reacts. Or ask a friend to startle you after you have forgotten the request. What happens? Shoulders up, every muscle is contracted. This posture is not conducive to delivering a forceful and convincing message.

To avoid this hunched up position, your neck and shoulder muscles must be at ease. Practice the Body Work exercise until it becomes second nature. (It's also good for traffic jams and travel mishaps.)

Put your hands together waist high and push one palm again the other. Contract your arm, hand and diaphragm muscles and push as hard as you can. Hold for a count of six. Release and let hands fall loosely to your sides. Shake your hands freely. Repeat five times.

For maximum effect, this exercise should be done just before you begin speaking. Since pressing your hands together may look like you are praying for deliverance, you may want to try a variation. If you are seated, press your palms against the side edges of your chair. If you are standing while waiting to be introduced, you can push your hands and arms into the sides of your body.

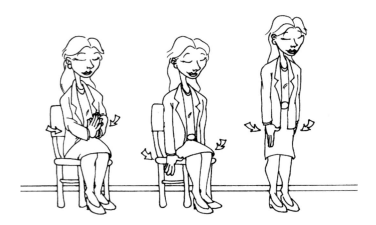

Use this exercise to relax.

The combination of contracting and releasing your muscles will free your neck and shoulders and allow you to relax while using your voice fully.

Brain Talk

Reframe and rephrase negative thoughts and comments into positive statements.

Generate a clear, positive image of yourself giving a powerful and successful presentation.

Sports psychologists and coaches have been using attitude modification and positive mental imagining for decades to improve athletic performances.

Now organizations are incorporating similar concepts under the name of "mind-set re-engineering."

In addition to requiring no additional equipment, you can practice brain talk anytime, anyplace, without detection.

Reframe your brain.

Here is how it works: Every time you begin to think or say something negative about your forthcoming presentation, stop and rephrase it positively. When someone asks, "Are you looking forward to the conference next week?" resist your gut reaction to spurt out, "I will never be ready in time. I am not good enough to be speaking on the same program with the vice president of sales. I will fall flat on my face."

Instead of reinforcing your fears and giving them substance, reframe and rephrase: "It's a challenge to be sharing the dais with Greg, and my new slant on logistics will be an eye-opener." (Then make sure it is!)

Generate positive images.

Watch a movie of your presentation in your head. See yourself being introduced. Watch as you stride to the front of the room. Notice how grounded you stand and how positive you look. Listen to your strong, well-modulated voice. The audience is responding positively — chuckling at your humor, enthralled with your story, mesmerized by your analysis. At the end, they break into tumultuous applause. This exercise will be more vivid if you know the room where you will be speaking and what you will be wearing. (If this suggestion sounds like a "new age" exercise, you may be interested to know that champion swimmers lie next to the pool and visualize every stroke of their 50-meter race before they begin. They also visualize that they will win and receive the gold medal. It is a proven way to improve performance.)

Now you have The 3 Bs. If you practice them until they become second nature, you will transform nervous tension into nervous energy. Be aware of the difference. You need that extra adrenaline flowing through your system to give an Olympian performance. You want that added "buzz" which gives you verve and vitality. You just need to be sure that those butterflies are flying in formation!

Positive Body Language

When you begin your speech, you want to establish a position which conveys your authority and ease. Being grounded looks good. But if you feel like moving around after fifteen seconds, do so! Walk across the stage, turn, look at the audience and share your first anecdote. (Check it out in advance. You don't want to fall off the edge of the platform.) At some point, you might want to move into the audience to ask a question and elicit their response. Remember: eyes like a moving target. Your audience will follow you avidly. When you cross the "invisible boundary" that separates speaker from audience, you make a strong statement that says, "I am the speaker, but I want to get closer to you because you are important to me."

Moving with purpose is the key! Every time you move to a new spot, stop and reground yourself. Spend at least ten seconds at the new place. I know this sounds rigid, but it helps you to exude power and comfort. A speaker who wanders around or constantly sways back and forth, soon convinces his audience he is as wishy-washy about his message as he is about his footwork.

Gesture with Ease

Use your hands and arms naturally. You may feel awkward using your hands when you are "on display" but if you work with a video camera and manage to catch yourself while you are explaining how to get to the conference center, you will see that you do use your hands to enhance and complete your words.

Consider investing in a practice session to polish your delivery. After all, if you want to improve your golf stance or your back-swing, you get pointers from a pro. Find a speech and communications consultant like me who works with video and get some personalized coaching.

A first-time client stood at the front of his conference room and read from a text, "Good morning, ladies and gentlemen." I could see this was going to be a classic case, so after two minutes, I politely stopped him and asked him to describe his favorite childhood activity. He stared at me blankly. I smiled encouragingly. (The video camera was running.) Hesitantly, he began to describe Cornwall on the south coast of Great Britain where he had spent hours exploring the river banks of King Arthur's territory. Spontaneously, he started gesturing. He even drew a map on the flip chart. Watching the video afterwards, he clearly saw that although he had started off giving a stiff-upper-lip presentation, as soon as he got involved, he moved and gestured naturally. His voice became more expressive. He was communicating. He threw away his prepared script and produced a presentation which both informed and involved his audience by using a pool table to explain polymers. He has since delivered his speech 18 times — each time with success.

Accept the challenge. Put yourself on videotape. Talk about your childhood. Tape yourself a second time and describe an experience where you were scared to death or a time when you were the center of attention and it felt good. I know you will want to resist, but it does help to get your emotions involved. Then analyze your posture, your smile, your eye contact, your stride and your gestures. Experiment. Exaggerate. Watching the video without the sound is an excellent and revealing exercise.

Remember that when you make a gesture, you need to follow through. If you drop your hands quickly to your sides instead of holding your pose for a second, it looks incomplete.

Using a mirror isn't ideal. Most of us are highly critical of what our mirrors show us about our bodies. If you can look at yourself naked in front of a full length mirror and smile, then you won't let the mirror give you only negative feedback. Use it to practice your gestures. Otherwise just use it to check for lipstick on your teeth or an open zipper.

Master Your Voice

Slow Down (At the Beginning)

As soon as the adrenaline starts flowing and the "fight or flight" reaction kicks in, most people start speaking faster. Even though our brains can process language more rapidly than most of us talk, an audience needs time to become accustomed to your voice.

Pauses Are Power!

A speaker who pauses effectively is in control.

- 💮 She starts with a pause which signals to the audience that as soon as their chit-chat subsides, the main event will get underway.
- 💮 She pauses to let the audience assimilate what she has just discussed.
- 💮 If she tells a light-hearted anecdote, she pauses for the ensuing ripple of laughter, and she pauses until it subsides.
- 💮 If two people in the third row begin talking to each other, she looks at them and pauses until they stop.
- 💮 She pauses for emphasis.
- 💮 When she is finished, she pauses for the applause that she will inevitably receive.

When pauses are accompanied with eye contact and a warm pleasant look, they are formidable. A pause is easy to execute: just stop and wait and look at the audience.

Project Your Voice with Energy!

If you remember to project your voice, you will be heard in most speaking situations. To practice, imagine that you are throwing a big rubber ball to the corner of the room. As it leaves your hands, call to an imaginary someone to catch the ball. Sense the words leaving your mouth and direct them to that imaginary person.

Another way to project your voice is to imagine that it is a strong beam of light searching into the back of the room. Let your voice guide that light.

Vary Your Pace and Pitch

A monotonous tone of voice that drones on is deadly for a speaker. You need to modulate your voice by varying the pace (faster and slower) and the pitch (higher and lower). When you are practicing your talk out loud (at least three times before you deliver your talk), figure out where to make some appropriate changes. Use a brisk pace to enliven your words and a more intimate tone to captivate your listeners.

Even an appealing voice will eventually lull an audience into dreamland. If you have ever driven a finely tuned, high-powered sports car down the highway, you know what I mean. Every once in a while you need a sharp curve or a bump in the road to jolt you into full attention. The same is true for your audience.

You can also "jolt" your audience by going very quiet. Besides which people tend to believe what you say when you whisper. Shh . . .

Articulate Clearly

Lots of people have "lazy lips." In actual fact, you need to get your lips, your tongue, teeth, lower jaw, hard and soft palate and your throat all working in order to form the sounds of speech.

Sloppy diction also needs to be eliminated. Pronounce words correctly instead of slurring them. Here are some words which native English speakers frequently mispronounce:

et cetera (not ec cetera)

sandwich (not samwich)

February (not Febuary)

government (not goverment)

Eliminate Filler Sounds like "Ya Know" and "And Um"

An effective way to rid yourself of saying useless sounds is to give a colleague a bag of marbles and an empty tin can. As you rehearse for a speech, your colleague drops a marble into the can every time you say the offending sound. I used this little gimmick to rid myself of exclaiming "absolutely" too frequently. Did it work? Absolutely.

Treat Your Voice Tenderly

Often speakers experience dry mouths and clamor for a glass of water. You can solve the problem by activating the saliva in your mouth. First gently bite the edges of your tongue with your teeth. Or, press your entire tongue to the bottom of your mouth and hold it there until the saliva flows. If you are a visual person, imagine that you are slicing a big juicy lemon and sucking the juice.

Before you begin your presentation, be kind to your voice. Avoid milk or creamy drinks which coat your throat. Keep your vocal apparatus moist by drinking slightly sweetened warm tea or diluted fruit juice.

If you sense that you are losing your voice, stop talking completely. Save your voice for your speech. You may feel foolish using a pad of paper to write notes, but the best thing you can do is to rest your voice. If you need to see a doctor, perhaps you can get a recommendation from a professional singer. In the meantime, do not even whisper.

What about drinking alcohol to "wet your whistle" and relax your nerves? I counsel my clients never to touch alcohol before speaking. The problem with alcohol is that one drink gives you a little confidence. The second drink gives you even more. Eventually you feel all-powerful which is a sure sign that your performance will be sloppy and incoherent. Save the alcohol until after you finish speaking.

If you have just read this chapter at one sitting, you may be ready to throw your hands up in dismay and wonder if you can ever change the habits of a lifetime. Of course you can. Goethe, who lived before indoor skating rinks and swimming pools said, "We learn to skate in the summer and swim in the winter." Take his message to heart and give yourself time to assimilate your new habits. If you are tolerant and forgiving of yourself, you will soon be able to deliver your message with comfort and power and will echo Li Chunghui who wrote me, "I'll never forget these techniques because they became a part of my body."

8

Handle Q&A Sessions, Hecklers and Other Situations with Ease

Speaking in the international business arena is exhilarating and rewarding but not without its perils. Some can be foreseen; others crop up when least expected.

Eliminating potential catastrophes is obviously your first priority. In Chapter 9, you will find an exhaustive checklist for preparing the conference room and equipment. Please use it. No one else cares quite as much (or will be quite as stuck) as you if the microphone doesn't work or the slides are out of order. Once you have checked out the equipment, you have to take into consideration the human element. You only need two whispering delegates or one heckler to put a dent into your well-prepared and thoroughly rehearsed presentation.

Experience has shown that no matter how many precautions you take, when calamity strikes, it will be at the most awkward moment and in the most embarrassing way. Certain things are always going to remain beyond your control, but you should have a contingency plan.

Get Good Mileage Out of Your Question and Answer Session

Whenever you open yourself up to questions, you are in potential danger because the interactive nature of Q & A sessions can work positively or negatively.

If audience involvement won't be particularly beneficial to either party, why put yourself under undue pressure? Eliminate the question and answer session. (If the organizers give you more time than you need for your presentation, tell them you don't want it.) Then just before you conclude, say, "We won't have a question and answer session, but if you do have a question, please look for me during the coffee break. Now, let me wrap up by saying . . ."

On the other hand, if you do want the audience to participate, you need a strong action plan to get them involved. This section is divided into two parts: questions and answers. Now who wants to ask the first question?

What if No One Asks a Question?

No one wants to ask the first question. That's because no one wants to stand out in a crowd. You can circumvent this dilemma. Before your presentation, ask someone who will be in your audience to get the ball rolling and give this person something to ask. For example, "Since I won't go into details about our expansion in the Middle East, you might ask me about that." (Then she can listen to your talk without constantly trying to formulate a clever question for afterwards.)

Another option is to raise your own hand and to ask confidently, "What questions may I answer?" Please notice the exact phrasing. "What questions may I answer?" You must assume that the audience has questions, several questions, in fact! Putting up your own hand encourages your audience to raise their hands. Wait at least five seconds with a friendly expression on your face. People need time to get their courage in gear. After five seconds, if no one responds, try this technique. With a smile on your face and enthusiasm in your voice, look at your audience and ask your own question, such as, "I'm often asked why I chose Chicago as my North American base."

After you answer your own question, look at the audience in a non-threatening way and say, "Now, what other questions may I answer?" Is it a gimmick? Yes. Does it work? Usually.

Someone Just Asked a Question. Now What?

Let's imagine that someone has asked a question. Now what do you do? Listen to what is really being asked. Sometimes the questioner only wants to make a good impression on someone else in the room.

Treat every question with respect and courtesy. If you say, "Every fool should know that milk freezes at a lower temperature than water," you alienate not only the person who asked the question, but also your entire audience who will feel empathy for their maligned compatriot.

If the question comes from the front row, you may need to say: "Before I answer this question, I want to make sure those of you in the back have heard it, so let me repeat it." Of course, when the question comes from the back row, you don't need to repeat it because if you heard it, so did everyone else. If you are being simultaneously interpreted and the questioner didn't use a microphone, you need to repeat the question so the interpreters can hear it.

If you don't understand the question, ask for clarification: "I didn't catch what you were asking. Would you please repeat it?" Or "I'm having difficulties in understanding this question (not 'this delegate' but 'this question') Can anyone help us out?"

Rephrase a negative question. Don't say, "You would like to know about our shoddy products and sweatshop working conditions . . ."

After one or two hesitant queries, you may be bombarded with questions. Try to keep track of the order. Avoid pointing your finger at anyone. If you need to gesture, graciously extend your arm and hand with the palm up. It might help to say, "After the woman in front, let's have a question from the man next to the window, and then the woman at the back."

I find it's useful and interesting to ask people to identify themselves by name and organization before they ask their questions. If you choose to take this approach, be sure that everyone follows suit.

And Now the Answers

Most speakers relish this stage of the game because a "one-to-one" feeling prevails. However, if you become too comfortable, you will lose the momentum which you have built up. As you answer, maintain a brisk and dynamic pace.

Feel free to answer just one part of a multi-pack question. Then if you don't want to answer the entire question, break eye contact with the questioner and look elsewhere for another question.

When you don't know the answer, admit it and add, "Please give me your business card, and I will get the answer to you by next week." In many Asian countries, admitting ignorance is a sensitive issue. Perhaps you can say, "I will check on those results and let you know next week."

Never say, "No comment." It has come to mean, "I am guilty, but I am keeping my mouth shut." Try to give a positive explanation, "We are completing our analysis, and we will have a clearer picture early next month."

If the question is inappropriate, deflect it and say, for example: "Let's stick to questions dealing with the financial aspects for now. But I will be happy to talk to you later about styling and colors."

Answer briefly and resist including new information unless it is absolutely necessary to make your point. You want to keep the pace flowing and then end at a high point. Even if you see some hands in the air, when your time is almost up, conclude: "What a pleasure this has been for me. Without a doubt, opening an office here in Delhi is our smartest move of the year. (Never forget to end by getting your major point across one more time.) So, when you want to make your next smart move, let Smart Moves do it for you."

When You Substitute for Another Speaker

Substituting for someone else is always problematic, but with the right attitude, you can usually turn someone else's misfortune into your good fortune. However, always consider the audience's point of view. If the indisposed speaker hasn't provided a manuscript, canceling may be the best decision all round.

Otherwise, you need to set a pleasant mood at the beginning. If you start with a brief explanation, you will put the audience's worries to rest: "It's unfortunate that Mr. Webster cannot be here today. I spoke with him just an hour ago, and he is recovering rapidly from his bout of food poisoning." If you go into details, the audience may focus on the missing speaker, not his message which you are delivering in his place.

Next, bridge to your unexpected good fortune at being able to address this distinguished audience: "Now it is my privilege to tell you about the world's most innovative company and our plans for expansion in this part of the world. As you know, we are looking for a partner. We're hoping that you are sitting in this very room."

Before you give Webster's speech, practice it out loud. You have to get your mouth around his words. Take a pencil and cross out anything that's awkward, but resist rewriting the speech at the last minute. Then practice it out loud.

Once you begin, enjoy yourself. Incorporate pauses, smile during the witty bits, comment on the slides. When you look comfortable and in command, the audience finds it easier to concentrate on the message.

If you are too poorly briefed to handle questions and answers, either enlist someone who can help or eliminate the question and answer session. (Tell the conference organizers in advance, of course.)

The After-Lunch Slot

If you get the after-lunch slot, consider telling the organizers you have an important meeting in another city right after lunch and will have to leave just before lunch. Otherwise, unless you want your audience to doze through your speech, you need to deliver a compelling message eloquently.

Here's one way to make the best of a poor situation. As soon as the delegates resume their seats, stand up and with a twinkle in your eye, say: "When I learned I would be addressing this distinguished audience just after lunch, I must admit I was a bit concerned. You see, I had just read a study about the worst time to give a presentation. You guessed it! Right after lunch. According to this study, the blood that should be activating your brain is busy digesting your food and 25 percent of you are already asleep."

If you are lucky, the other 75 percent will chuckle. Then if you keep your talk brief and punchy, you may keep your audience awake. If not, you will have learned an important lesson.

The After-Dinner Slot

The format for many conferences nowadays begins "the night before" with a reception and dinner. This enables participants to get a day's work done in some other city before arriving at the conference site and ensures they are on tap the following morning.

If you are asked to speak at such a dinner, it's important that you know whether you are meant to be giving an amusing postprandial talk or an earnest business presentation. Otherwise you and your audience might be at cross-purposes. They are expecting witty remarks while you are advocating increased sustainable architecture.

If your message is serious, you might suggest relocating in a conference room to ensure a properly serious mood. Even still, you are well-advised to forego a Question and Answer session. At this time of the evening, the interest level and attention span of many of your listeners will be minimal.

Read a Script Convincingly: Use the Scoop Technique

The major risks of reading from a manuscript are that you sound stilted and that your eyes are glued to the paper instead of making contact with your audience. These drawbacks can be greatly diminished if you learn how to use The Scoop Technique. First, check your written text carefully and reword it so that it sounds the way you speak. Make the sentences short and use active verbs. Let your voice supply emphasis, pauses, changes in intensity and punctuation marks. Hear the differences:

Written language: At the heart of this market penetration is a clear and unwavering commitment to research and development.

Spoken: We are committed to research and development.

Practice the Scoop Technique.

Written: Following the reduction of our involvement in the more cyclical primary side of our product, we have pointed our wide array of technological and manufacturing expertise towards the transportation markets.

Spoken: We've reduced our involvement in the more cyclical side. Now we're pointing our technological and manufacturing expertise towards new markets.

Since most texts are produced on computers, changing the type face and font size is a breeze. If you put your script into the format shown in Figure 8.1, it will be much easier to read. (If you are at the age where your eyesight is failing, enlarging the text will eliminate the need for reading glasses.)

❧ Scoop up a phrase, then look at the audience and say it.

❧ Only speak when your eyes are up.

❧ Practice the entire speech out loud at least twice.

This technique takes time to learn, but once you have mastered it, you will be able to deliver any written speech naturally and really connect with your audience.

Audience Interference

Sometimes just a few people threaten to take over a conference. They may not do it intentionally. Perhaps one person is interpreting for her neighbor's benefit. If you hear two people in the sixth row talking to each other in increasingly louder voices, what do you do? The best tactic is to move next to them and look at them pointedly. Often this is enough to dissuade them from speaking. If you discover that one person is explaining to her neighbor, say in a friendly voice, "I realize that you are trying to be helpful, but your voices are distracting us. Let's meet later and I will explain the main points of my talk."

What if the interference comes from your boss who stands up and interrupts you in the middle of your presentation? My suggestion would be to slow down and say, "I appreciate your support, Mr. Meddler, and I would hope you would let me finish. The audience isn't as well informed as we are, and they need to get the whole picture."

FIGURE 8.1 The Scoop Technique

To use **The Scoop Technique** successfully, set up the text like this page. (Font at least size 22.)

Begin each sentence on a new line.

Never carry over part of a sentence to the next page.

<u>Underline</u>, CAPITALIZE or type important points in **bold**.

In the margin, write "PAUSE," draw happy faces as friendly reminders.

Highlight with color.

Keep the lower third of the page free.

Number the pages.

Once completed, avoid changing the script.

Ignoring a distraction rarely makes it disappear. If you are disturbed by something, your audience will be, too. Much better to deal with it and then get on with your speech.

When Your Audience Is Unreceptive

If you have done your audience analysis, you know whether to emphasize what you have in common or to admit your differences and then bridge to mutual concerns.

> When addressing The International Sugar Organization, Hans Heezen started by reviewing trends in the world of sweetness which affected both the sugar and the intense sweetener industries. He showed that growth was possible for both sugar and intense sweeteners and suggested: "Let us stop fighting. There's room for all of us. Let us work together to promote the enjoyment of sweet taste."
>
> He then presented an idea where both sugar and aspartame could benefit by joining forces. In conclusion, he said, "I don't have the illusion that you will all contact me right after this meeting and say, 'let's start working together,' but if we can create more demand for sweetness and cooperate where and when this makes sense, the future will be sweet for all of us."
>
> In wrapping up the entire conference the moderator reinforced Hans's message and said, "I like the words we heard from Hans Heezen — we have to work together."

Now that's a winning result.

Hecklers in the Audience

Audience members who maliciously heckle a speaker are rarely found in a business audience. Nevertheless, it pays to be prepared. As soon as you recognize that you are in potential danger of unwanted interference, continue with your speech as you move to where the hecklers are seated and confront them with a look that says, "I am speaking now. Please allow me to continue." Usually that will suffice. However, if the hecklers try to engage you in a debate, dismiss them curtly but with equanimity, "We have different opinions, and I have been asked to give mine at this point." Then break eye contact and ignore them. If you want to tackle the situation with humor, you could look at them with a knowing smile and say, "I know who you are. I have seen you on television. You're called 'interference.'"

Usually your audience will be on your side. As a last resort, state the situation and let the facts speak for themselves: "It's impossible for me to continue with these interruptions. Perhaps those of you who would like to hear me should move to the front of the room. Or we could relocate or reschedule." If the audience doesn't come to your assistance, bow out graciously. Try hard to remain composed. You rarely have much to gain by stooping to the level of your detractors, and you may have much to lose. Everyone will remember your emotional outburst long after they have forgotten that it was justified.

Emergencies

When you are standing in front of an audience, they put you in command, at least psychologically. If someone faints, you are expected to take charge. Even if you are not from the local area, people will hope that you know how to proceed. Check out in advance who is in charge of the event (often the conference moderator) and who the on-site manager is. If someone has a seizure, you may have to say: "The gentleman in the third row seems to be having a seizure. Would someone please inform Ms. Benz, the banqueting manager at once. Is there a qualified medical person here who could help? Everyone else, please remain seated."

> I once moderated an event where many audience members could not see another group seated in another area. When a woman collapsed, I kept one eye on the emergency area to see that it was being dealt with competently. In this case, I did not mention the crisis for fear of arousing undue concern in the people who could not see what was happening. Later, when I was given a note on the woman's condition, I said, "Earlier this evening, the warm temperature in the banquet hall affected one of our guests who is now recovering well. For more information, please see me afterwards. And now, let us continue."

If it's a fire or flood, ask your audience to follow the instructions found in the seat pockets in front of them. No, seriously, the best insurance is being prepared for all contingencies. No matter what happens you should remain calm, collected and in control. In many true life emergencies, it is the panic which causes the most problems.

If Your Audience Is Falling Asleep

If your audience is falling asleep, you need to open some windows or get them on their feet. If you are addressing a group containing Americans, ask them to demonstrate a "seventh-inning stretch." It's almost certain they will comply because Americans enjoy audience participation. Then suggest, "How about everyone taking a seventh-inning stretch!" (Baseball games have nine innings. By the seventh inning, most viewers need to stand up and take the kinks out of their joints, hence the "seventh-inning stretch.") In other cultures you may have to be more subtle.

> At a marketing conference where the two previous speakers had lulled the audience into a state of numbness, the president of a major airline used this ploy to effect. He began by asking, "How many of you have flown to Asia in the last six months? Please stand up." (Twenty percent of his audience stood up.) He continued, "Would those of you who have traveled to North America now stand up." (Another 50 percent stood up.) "How many have flown to Latin America . . . oh, why doesn't everyone stand up. You've been in a holding pattern long enough. Take a deep breath and stretch. Great! Now get comfortable while I tell you about our new business class features."

Video Conferences and Conference Calls

With the advent of sophisticated video technology, some pundits predicted that live conferences would vanish. Although recent global events and restricted budgets have curtailed face-to-face exchanges, it appears that we human beings still prefer to rub elbows and shake hands whenever we can.

Speaking via satellite at an international conference:

If you are called upon to speak to a conference via satellite, remember that the technology transmitting your image across thousands of miles deadens even the most congenial face. You need to be incredibly warm and engaging. The larger the screen, the more you have to imagine you are speaking to that one important person who needs to hear your message. (Quite a challenge when you are in TV studio in Copenhagen addressing two hundred immunologists who are seated in a lecture hall in Boston.)

Although your natural charm and warmth are not adequately projected on large video screen, your face is magnified. Your nose may be six feet high. Personal grooming is a must. Check for stray hairs, spinach between your teeth, messy lipstick. If an on-site makeup artist offers to give you a dusting of neutral powder, accept it. Or do it yourself. You don't want the glare from your sweating brow or balding head to outshine your message.

Try to schedule a dry run so you can get used to the camera.

Timing is crucial. Satellite time is purchased at great expense, so you need to ensure that your entire message is transmitted while your audience is still on-line.

When I moderated the Zurich session of an international symposium originating in New York, we missed the grand finale because the New York group did not keep to the schedule and our previously reserved time segment expired. Although it was 5 p.m. in New York, it was already 11 p.m. in Switzerland as 150 weary and disgruntled delegates departed with an incomplete take-home message.

Speaking via satellite to your clients and customers:

When speaking to your customers in Japan, it's wise to observe their dress code which is dark jacket, white shirt and conservative tie. You want to make a serious impression, and you cannot know where and to whom your video will be shown. (Check the Country Profiles for each country's dress code.)

Internal company video conferences:

Your meeting needs a well-prepared and publicized agenda. Make sure that all participants receive a copy in advance. At the start, introduce yourselves. Particularly Americans may try to forego this formality, but international participants take a little longer to get warmed up. Everyone needs to attach a name to a face and/or voice, especially if it is a conference call (using an audio link). Usually the information is assessed simultaneously by all parties over an intranet or internet link which the presenter controls. The lack of visual contact makes it easy for people to interrupt and disrupt the communication flow. Additionally, cultural differences come into play. Participants whose native language is not English may be reluctant to offer comments. If twenty participants are in Dallas and one is in Helsinki, the isolated person needs to be included. A friendly and firm moderator ensures that the call stays on track and allows everyone a chance to contribute.

Now why don't you stand up before continuing with the next chapter. And stretch!

CHAPTER

9

Set Up for Speaking Success

John Naisbitt, author of Megatrends Asia, addressed a prestigious group of 250 Swiss bankers at a five-star Zurich hotel. Having just arrived on a 13-hour flight from Shanghai, he was dehydrated and asked for two glasses of plain water. The banquet manager brought him one long-stemmed glass of sparkling water. Naisbitt had specified normal water because it is easier to swallow when you are speaking. He had asked for two glasses because a tall glass wouldn't fit on the narrow shelf of the lectern. He finally got what he wanted, but unless you are a pro like John Naisbitt, an incident like this can tax your nerves and undermine your self-confidence.

Have you ever used someone else's office for a day? Where's the stapler? How do you adjust the heating? Have you ever cooked in a strange kitchen? Where's the garlic press? How does the grill function?

Little inconveniences won't keep you from preparing a report or a meal, but wouldn't it be easier if you knew where things were and how they operated?

That is why you need to check out the room and equipment in advance. Do it yourself. (If the sound system breaks down while you are speaking, you won't be as disconcerted if you have your glass of water.)

When you are giving a speech in a country where people speak a different language, you need to be doubly sure that everything is under control. How do you get the staff to adjust the air conditioning? What's the word for extension cord in Arabic? The more you set the stage, the more comfortable you will be while you are speaking.

Room Size

If the room seats 200 and only 30 people are expected, rope off the back of the room or everyone will sit there. Otherwise explain, "We'll get more out of this session if we aren't so spread out. Please move forward." You can guarantee that your audience complies if you say, "Please stand." Then ask them to move forward.

A room filled to capacity is ideal. If, however, the room is a bit crowded, the audience will think, "Not an empty seat! This speaker must be good."

Tables/Seating Arrangement

Seats should be positioned so you can see all audience members.

A horseshoe or U-formation is the best arrangement to encourage interaction.

If your audience should be taking notes, tables (plus paper and pens) should be provided.

If you keep several vacant chairs near the entrance, latecomers will not stumble around to find a seat.

Decor

It helps to know the color of the walls and curtains, so that you and your clothes don't blend into the background. When you are giving a presentation, you want to stand out.

Platforms

If you are speaking in a large room with the audience seated on one level (at a banquet, for instance), a raised platform of at least 12 inches and preferably 20 inches will increase your visibility enormously. You need to make arrangements in advance, since a platform needs to be moved and installed.

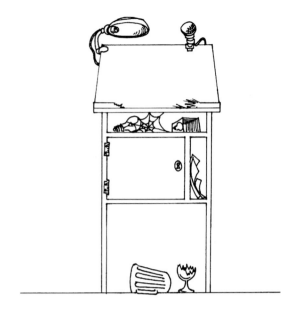

Most lecterns are barricades.

Lectern

At most hotels and conference centers, the lectern is a huge, unwieldy fortress which you can get lost behind. The reading light either doesn't work or casts a ghostly light on your face. The ledge which holds your notes is so low that you have to stoop to read them. If you attempt to place your notes up higher, they slide back down. The microphone is inevitably at an angle where you have to cock your head to speak into it. And forget about a convenient place to put a glass of water.

You may have to improvise to get your lectern in good working order. Ask for a light bulb that works or a standing lamp. Wedge a piece of wood at the bottom lip of the ledge to raise your papers up to reading level. Tape some carpet or a towel on the slanted part so that your notes don't slip down.

Better yet, avoid using a lectern. It is really a barrier between you and your audience. If you are reading, at least begin by standing next to it. Let the audience get a good look at you from head to toe. (To read a manuscript well, see "The Scoop Technique" in Chapter 8.)

Glass of Water

If you want a glass of water, get it in advance. Open the bottle and fill the glass and put it somewhere sensible.

The Lighting

Let there be light. If the speaker before you showed slides in a darkened room, ask that the blinds be opened before you begin. If, however, your conference room overlooks the swimming pool, you may want to keep the shades partially closed.

Find out if the lights can be dimmed and how the switches work. Even if you are using slides, the room doesn't have to be pitch black.

When the rest of the room is dark, you should be seen. Ask for a spotlight to illuminate you while you enlighten your audience. Do not underestimate the importance of having light on your face, especially when you are speaking in a multi-lingual situation. The more clearly we see your face, the better we understand your message.

Temperature/Ventilation

As a room fills up with people, it will heat up, so have the room cool and freshly aired when you begin. If you are speaking after lunch, be sure the room is aired during lunch. A stuffy room is an invitation to doze off, especially after a meal.

Distractions

Interruptions like sudden piped-in music or a ringing telephone at the back of the room can be prevented with forethought. No matter how many precautions you take, something may go wrong. If a car alarm goes off or a stranger stumbles into the room looking for another meeting, acknowledge disruptions calmly: "Let's not let that noise interfere with our meeting." or "This is the symposium on global warming." If you take intrusions in stride, so will your audience.

The Microphone

The most convenient type of microphone is the cordless variety. You attach the microphone to your lapel and put the battery pack in a pocket or hook it to your belt. (Women need to wear a jacket or dress with a pocket.)

Battery microphones operate on special frequencies. An outside source like an electric tram, model airplane, or a cellular phone network can cause interference. If that happens, turn off the battery mic and grab one that is plugged in. Always check that a stand-by microphone is operating.

Test the microphone (either before the conference begins or during the coffee break before you speak.) Locate the on/off switch. If it is a stationary microphone, learn how to adjust the stand and note how long the cable is. Find someone to help you do a sound check. (You cannot do it alone.)

If you are using a portable microphone, hold it just under your mouth, like an ice cream cone and direct your voice to the farthest corner of the room. Remember that a microphone amplifies but does not improve your

Hold the microphone like an ice cream cone.

voice. You still need to articulate and project with energy. Ascertain how far you can turn your head and still be heard.

If your voice carries well without the mic, you may decide not to be amplified. However, human bodies absorb sound so when the hall is full, your voice will not project as well. If in doubt, use the mic.

One of the most annoying disturbances for both audience and speaker is a shrill whistling noise called feedback. It is often caused when the microphone gets too close to the loudspeakers, so if you are walking and talking, stay clear of them. You can check this out in advance.

In-House Technician

The best guarantee that nothing goes wrong is to know the name and pager number of the in-house technician!

Speaker's Checklist for Success

Complete and send your Speaker's Checklist for Success to the person responsible for your arrangements (see Figure 9.1). (If these organizers send you a form, check that everything crucial for the success of your talk is included.)

Your Appearance: You Are Your Best Visual Aid!

Think of yourself as your primary visual aid. You need to look your best. Make sure that your image supports your message. Wear something appropriate and attractive. Dress appropriately for the audience and for the occasion. When in doubt, be a bit too formal rather than too casual. As mentioned earlier, don't blend into the surroundings. In a oak-paneled conference room, don't wear brown. If you buy a new suit or dress for the occasion, break it in and check for wrinkling beforehand. As a speaker, make sure the audience's attention is not diverted by what you are or are not wearing.

Check the Country Profiles for the dress code in the country where you are speaking.

FIGURE 9.1 Speaker's Checklist for Success

Speaker's Checklist for Success

Name of speaker: _____

Speaker's title and firm: _____

Address: _____

Daytime phone: _____ Fax: _____

Speaking event: _____

Topic/title: _____

Who else is on the program: _____

Date of presentation: _____

List of who will be in the audience: _____

Time slot: _____ Time allotted: _____

Location of event: _____

Complete address: _____

Name of on-site contact person: _____

Telephone: _____ Fax: _____

Directions supplied: _____

Transportation: _____

Lodging: _____

Fees/expenses: _____

The Room

Chairs/tables: number and arrangement _____

What is the decor? _____

Lectern: _____

Lighting/light on speaker: _____

Temperature/Ventilation: _____

Equipment

Microphone: _____

Slide projector: _____

Overhead projector: _____

Video equipment: _____

Extension cables: _____

Flip chart: _____

Other: _____

Men:

- ❀ Choose high contrast colors for a platform presentation. A white shirt, a dark suit, and a bold tie send a strong message.

- ❀ Button your jacket before you walk to the front of the room.

- ❀ Polish your shoes: when you are standing on a platform, they are noticeable.

- ❀ Wear over-the-calf socks to avoid exposing bare leg when seated on a platform.

- ❀ Have everything you wear clean and pressed.

- ❀ Check for frayed collars and missing buttons.

- ❀ Get a haircut several days in advance.

- ❀ Avoid a "five o'clock shadow." If need be, make arrangements to shave before you speak.

- ❀ Bring along an extra shirt if you perspire profusely.

Women:

- ❀ Chapter 10 has more guidelines about dress and grooming for women.

Many of the above tips are really just a matter of good common sense, but frequently speakers ignore the most obvious things when they are getting ready to speak.

Travel Tips for Speakers

When you travel by air, do not check in your laptop, CD-ROMs with your slides, script or the tie you plan to wear. Put them in your hand luggage.

For added security, send one set of materials in advance, take one set with you and leave another at your office to be courier expressed if the first two disappear.

Since you may be traveling across several time zones to an unfamiliar city where people speak a foreign language, you need to treat your global speaking assignment with respect. Sandwiching it between a client conference and a courtesy call will not do justice to your message, your audience or you.

Be extra kind to yourself. Giving a major presentation is energy-consuming so give yourself a day to get used to the high altitude or the humid weather. As you walk to the front of the auditorium, you will realize that it pays to be in good form.

❧ Arrive early.

❧ Get lots of fresh air.

❧ If you exercise at home, exercise here.

❧ Eat lightly and drink moderately.

❧ Get to bed early. You can celebrate the night after you have spoken.

CHAPTER

10

Raise Your Voice: Guidelines for Women

A woman walked to the front of the room to accept The Management Symposium Achievement Award. On her way up the steps, she stumbled and fell onto the stage. She picked herself up and walked to the lectern. As she looked at the audience and took a deep breath, a luminous smile lit up her face. She said in a clear voice, "Sometimes you also stumble when you're climbing the ladder to success." Three hundred women burst into applause!

Women face stumbling blocks in the international business arena. Men do, too, of course, but in this chapter I'm directing my voice especially to women. So if you need some encouragement to raise your voice and some guidelines on how to do it, please "listen up."

Speaking in the public forum is a great way for a woman to get visibility, earn credibility, and advance her career. And it is a splendid way to gain personal fulfillment. If you have doubts about your ability to speak effectively in front of a group, that is perfectly understandable. Traditionally women have not been encouraged to speak up. In fact, for generations women have been appreciated for maintaining soft voices and low profiles. Instead of making policy, they have been making beds, making lunches, making do.

Now is the time to start making changes. Right now, take a deep breath and realign your attitude. Imagine you are standing at the front of a conference room. All eyes are on you. You wait quietly until a hush comes over the room. Confidently you begin to speak. Your voice is resonant and expressive. Your message has a compelling urgency that keeps your audience's

Sometimes you stumble . . .

attention. You can see the interest in their faces as your well-chosen words inform, delight and persuade. You gesture with assurance and move with ease. You feel comfortable and in control. As you end with clarity and conviction, your audience bursts into applause. You return to your seat and silently congratulate yourself. You have succeeded!

Would you like to be such a speaker? What is stopping you? Your background, your gender, your voice, your nerves?

Turning the above scenario into reality requires more than a vivid imagination, but never underestimate the power of affirming and imagining your goal. Get rid of negative and energy-sapping doubts.

Accept and use what makes you special and target other areas for improvement. As the popular song says, "You've got to accentuate the positive, eliminate the negative, latch on to the affirmative, but don't mess with Mr. In-between."

You may know a "Mr. In-between." Whenever you take a false step or make a blunder, he rolls his eyes, shakes his finger and gloats, "typical woman."

Let's turn the phrase "typical woman" into an accolade of the highest order instead of an insult. Let's start right now.

Surpass Expectations:
Be Focused, Organized and Punctual

When you stand at the speaker's lectern, you have to be aware that your audience's expectations will be high. Do not disappoint them. Since women are occasionally perceived as being vague and disorganized, your presentation needs to be highly focused and well organized. Since women have the reputation for always being late, you need to be on time.

Be Focused

Addressing the first North American Greening Roofs Conference which was hosted by Chicago, Kimberly Worthington of the city's Environment Department was professional, factual and focused. She explained how the city had convinced its citizens of the benefits of green roofs. She said, "In Chicago, if we haven't seen it, we don't believe it. So we started at the top— on the rooftop of City Hall, to be exact." Systematically, Kimberly described how the 20,300 square-foot rooftop garden was created. Then she continued, "Chicagoans said, 'The rooftop garden looks great, but does it have any positive effect?' Yes, it does! We can show that green roofs improve the microclimate and save energy because we are monitoring the temperatures atop City Hall and the adjacent County Building. In fact, on August 9, 2001 at 1:45 p.m., with air temperature over 90°F, temperatures on the Rooftop Garden were 100°F compared to 170° on the surface of the neighboring County Building. We now have 43 green roof projects underway and are committed to making Chicago the greenest city in the country."

Be Organized

In addition to being well-organized, you might find it judicious to include phrases like the following:

- ❂ "first let's get a comprehensive overview"
- ❂ "having thoroughly analyzed the second reason"
- ❂ "continuing in a logical way "
- ❂ "considered rationally"
- ❂ "let's put this into a coherent framework"

Once you have analyzed your audience, you may decide to throw in some masculine lingo to get your message across. I am not advocating this approach, but it's a jungle out there. While you're jockeying for position, you need to keep your eye on the ball and take no hostages. (Can you find the male-talk expressions?)

Be Punctual

Even when you are speaking in a country or culture where time is considered flexible, do everything in your power to start and finish punctually. You may even want to casually comment that "we're right on time." Since women are often perceived as running late, your audience needs to know that you consider their time (and yours) precious.

Use On-Target Language

Dispense with those tag questions at the end of your sentences, you know what I mean? Those little additions make you sound indecisive, don't you agree? (See what I mean?)

Get rid of the harmless but useless qualifying words which are intended to soften the communication process. Instead of saying, "We probably ought to maybe consider thinking about a slight modification of that procedure which is really more or less adequate" say, "We need to change the procedure."

Begin sentences with the word "I." As in, "I think we need to change the procedure."

If you want to get ahead on the speaker's platform (and in your career), stop apologizing for things that you are not responsible for. If the speaker before you doesn't show up, don't tell the audience, "I am sorry we have to change things." Instead say, "The speaker scheduled for 10 a.m. is not here, so I will deliver my presentation now."

Be Sensitive to Your Audience

Women have an innate sensitivity to relationships and social interaction. This is an invaluable attribute when it comes to addressing an audience. First, you really do want to make a connection. Secondly, you have the ability to do so.

Once you have tailored your speech for your special audience, maintain rapport by keeping your "antennae" out during your presentation. Listen with your eyes.

Most women can switch operating modes in a split second. Use your "people skills." If you see puzzled faces, do not hesitate to explain something again in different words. Then, to defuse possible criticism that you have repeated yourself, you can say casually, "Sometimes it's better the second time around."

Surprise Your Audience: Enjoy Yourself

One of the nicest things you can do is to let your audience know you are enjoying yourself. And, of course, if you have prepared and are in control of the situation, you should be enjoying yourself. You are sharing your experience, your research, your ideas with a group of interested and receptive human beings. What could be nicer?

Many women speakers need to be coaxed to smile, to exude warmth and enthusiasm. Why? Because they are afraid they will not be taken seriously. Why must seriousness be equated with grimness?

As dancer Margot Fonteyn said, "The one important thing I have learned is the difference between taking one's work seriously and taking one's self seriously. The first is imperative and the second is disastrous." Show your audience that you understand the difference. Include a comment or personal anecdote which reveals the lighter side of your life.

Include a "Chuckler"

Early in your presentation, give your audience a glimpse of yourself by including a "chuckler." Laughter breaks the ice and builds connections. More importantly, it relaxes both you and your audience. Literally. That's why it pays to have a "disarming smile." One of my speeches is titled "Take the Mess Out of Your Message." My opening words always get a smile, sometimes even a chuckle. I begin by saying, "When I asked my son what he thought about the title of this speech, he raised his eyebrows and said (as only a teenager can), 'Mom, if you take the "mess" out of your message, all you have left is "age," and I thought you didn't like to mention yours!'" I allow my audience to see that I like sharing my son's wit with them.

Channel Your Nerves

I don't know if women get more nervous than men do, but they talk about it more. Admitting that you are nervous is all right, as long as you don't admit it to your audience.

The absolutely best way to alleviate nerves is by being incredibly well prepared. I have said it before, and I shall say it again. Nothing beats preparation.

Once you have voiced your fears, stop repeating yourself. Start imagining what a superb job you will do on the day. If you don't have anyone around to give you verbal encouragement, give it to yourself. When you get a little jumpy at the prospect of speaking to 200 people, tell yourself, "I will do a good job. The audience will like my speech. They will chuckle at the light-hearted bits. I will be the best speaker at the conference."

Channel your nerves.

Listen to Your Voice

If you shy away from listening to yourself, perhaps you don't like what you hear. The little voice inside your head can sabotage you if you let it. Maybe you need to tell that negative, complaining voice to go away.

Years ago, driving down the coast of France, I kept hearing a voice criticizing me for my poor driving, my hopeless sense of direction and my inability to read a French road sign. Suddenly I pulled off the road and addressed that voice in my head. I told her to mind her own business. Now, whenever she tells me that I am incompetent or stupid, I tell her to get lost. And she does. What a relief to get rid of the voice that holds you back. What a release to find the voice that moves you on. You need to believe that you can succeed. You need to believe that it is all right to succeed. That true inner voice is the one you need to start sharing with your audience. You don't have to come on so strong that you send shock waves through the auditorium. Even a pebble thrown into a pool creates a ripple effect. Think of that pebble as your voice.

Increase Your Vocal Power

Once you start exploring how to utilize your voice optimally to express your inner voice, you will see how expressive and persuasive you can be. Your voice can open new doors for you.

Speaking of your voice, do you like it? Your voice is your vocal calling card. It ought to reflect you accurately and expressively. If you would like to make a change or two, why not start now.

Get Your Breath

Breathing is all-important. You need an adequate and sustained source of energy coming from the bottom of your lungs to push those words out of your mouth. The only way you can get that energy is to learn how to breathe deeply.

Strange, isn't it? That we have to re-learn a process crucial for our survival. Perhaps it is the enormous stress in our lives, but many people need breathing lessons. Whatever the cause, start taking the time to breathe deeply. Find a time and a place to sit quietly or lie on the floor and just breathe. You must be relaxed and open. Free yourself from unnecessary tension. Breathe out and in. Quietly. Deeply. Naturally.

Lower Your Pitch

Many women clients complain their voice is too high. A lower pitched voice is more pleasant to listen to and carries more authority.

Your voice's pitch is partially determined by the length and width of the vocal cords which are thickish bits of muscle fiber that work as a valve. They vibrate in the production of sound. The process is infinitely complex, but that's the general concept. Women's vocal cords are shorter and narrower than men's which is why our natural pitch is higher.

When you get nervous, the added tension contracts the vocal cords and raises the pitch of your voice even more. So it pays to stay calm. Think "slow and low." In addition to which, pitch is also determined by imitation. If your mother and the other women in your formative years had high-pitched voices, you probably have copied them. In some societies having a high-pitched voice is socially acceptable for a woman, and signals femininity.

If you want to project a stronger image, find yourself a new role model. You may want to buy an audiotape of a woman whose voice you like and listen to it. Then you can consciously practice speaking with a lower pitch. In the film *Working Girl*, a secretary (Melanie Griffith) copies her boss (Sigourney Weaver) by listening to her Dictaphone. Once she eliminates her strident New York accent and starts speaking with more authority and power, Melanie cracks the glass ceiling wide open. (She ends up with an office of her own and Harrison Ford.)

First you need to hear how low your voice can go. Imagine that you are moving your voice from the top of your head to your throat area and then into your chest. Begin at your normal pitch saying, "Let's learn how low I can go." Repeat the sentence and drop your voice until you can go no lower. If you place your hand on your breastbone, you can check to see that you are creating chest cavity resonance.

Start speaking using one of these lower notes as your "base." The most difficult thing about lowering the pitch of your voice is to get into the new habit of speaking lower. If you put a sign near your telephone "Speak Low," you will be reminded to consciously lower your voice when you are on the phone. Practicing on the phone has the added advantage that most people will not be aware of what you are doing.

Articulate Clearly

In all speaking situations, you need to speak with a well-tuned vocal apparatus. Say a sentence or two with your mouth wide open. Now yawn gently and open your mouth twice as wide. Say the sentences again and use your tongue, lips and teeth in an exaggerated way to articulate the words. You don't want to do this in public, but you need to feel what it is like to get your mouth around the sounds you are saying. If you practice by using tongue twisters, nursery rhymes, or stock quotations from the newspaper, you will soon hear how much crisper your diction is.

Project Your Voice

Many women have been raised to speak softly and demurely. If as a girl you were encouraged to smile sweetly, tilt your head and say with eyebrows raised, "Really?" then it is no wonder that you find it difficult to get your words heard. Really! The easiest way to project your voice is to "speak out." It's what you do naturally in your daily life. If you see some friends about to disappear around the corner, you can aim your voice directly so that it catches their attention. Practice aiming your voice at different distances.

When you speak in public, you have to be able to project your voice for 30 minutes. That requires adequate breath and practice. Make a point of talking to different people in your audience. Pause. Keep your jaw relaxed. You can do it!

Pause for Power

Knowing when not to speak also opens new doors. Women often ramble on because they don't like the "sound of silence" and want to fill those uncomfortable gaps in a conversation. But in the business world, you may learn that the less you say, the more people listen.

Of course, on the speaker's platform, you are the only person speaking, but don't make it a non-stop monologue. Incorporate pauses wherever you can. Before you say your first word. Pause. Before you say something riveting. Pause. After you have said something provocative. Pause. When the audience laughs. Pause. When you need to catch your breath. Pause. When you want to recapture your audience's attention. Pause. Just for the fun of it. Pause.

Remember, the person who controls the silence, controls the room. Pause. (You will read about pauses elsewhere in *Speaking Globally*. Repetition is useful in communication.)

Connect with Your Eyes

Numerous studies show that women do not establish eye contact as often or as forcibly as men do. Whereas in a one-to-one conversation, you may find it difficult or undesirable to hold your own, when you are at the lectern, you do need to look at your audience. Remember the only way you can "listen" to their reactions is by looking at them.

When you look into the audience, really connect with them. In the course of your presentation, try to look at as many people as you can. If you get a positive look back from someone (and you usually will), then maintain eye contact for a few seconds before switching to someone else. If you get no feedback, don't let it bother you. Just look at someone else or glance at your notes.

Although you may think of smiling as something you do with your mouth, your eyes are also involved. Let your eyes sparkle with life and warmth. Just because many men have learned to deal with their stagefright by adopting a "poker face" doesn't mean you need to follow suit.

Stand and Move with Poise

Watch how you stand. Often women stand with one hip raised and one leg bent. You need to stand on your own two feet, literally and figuratively. Those feet need to be grounded at the beginning of your speech and when you are standing still. When you do change your position, your stride needs to be confident and assured. Don't be in a hurry. No slouching either. A steady measured pace projects power.

Tentative little gestures undermine your message. Use your hands and arms expansively. In fact, take up as much room as you can with your body. Claiming space gives you added presence. When you have raised your arms to say, "We need to include all of you," don't drop them immediately to your sides afterwards. You need to hold the position and release your pose gradually.

A tall investment banker stood at the front of the room. During her entire speech she hardly moved a muscle. Her voice was strained, and her body was tense. She looked like an archer with a stretched bow and arrow that was frozen in time. She controlled her voice, her body and her emotions but at an enormous cost to herself and to her audience who felt ill at ease in her presence.

Later, as we worked together, she explained that her parents had sent her to ballet lessons to learn how to carry herself well instead of slumping the way some tall women do. She had decided that moving and gesturing gracefully was not correct behavior for a banker. That is why she decided to do nothing at all. As soon as she gave herself permission to "spread her wings," she was commanding on the stage. Expansive movements suited her and increased her credibility.

I have another client who never moves when she speaks. Interestingly, she is also a banker. But the result is quite different. With her feet well planted on the floor, all the energy in her body seems to filter its way up to her face. When she speaks, her face is wonderfully animated. She radiates confidence and authority. She keeps her hands quietly at her sides or held effortlessly at waist level. She mesmerizes her audiences with quiet grace.

In today's frenetically-paced world, you can go almost anywhere and command both attention and respect when you move with poise. You signal that you are composed and self-assured.

So don't rush. Whether you are approaching the lectern or entering a roomful of strangers, slow down and move with grace and dignity. When you reach your destination, stand still. Look around you with an expression that says, "I know who I am." If you are poised, you will be able to handle the social functions which surround the conference scene. Even still, you may decide that delivering a speech is less intimidating and more rewarding than searching for a place to sit at the buffet lunch or circulating at a reception where you are expected to make small talk while balancing a glass in one hand and exchanging business cards with the other.

Take Advantage of Your Appearance

As a speaker in the international business arena, being a woman is an advantage in itself. You act and sound different from men. You look better in a skirt. Just imagine an international conference. After four male speakers in suits and ties, your audience will notice when you are heading to the lectern.

Yes, of course, you want to be remembered for your message, but first your audience has to remember who you are. And as a woman, you stand out. Take advantage of it. As the oft-quoted saying goes, "You never get a second chance to make a first impression."

A write-up in the newspaper rarely mentions a man's appearance whereas Elizabeth Dole's "slender calves" and "emerald contact lenses" are mentioned in an article in The Financial Times that then goes on to describe her as "resplendent in royal blue silk against the earth tones of a New England autumn." Mentioning physical attributes and wardrobe may be demeaning, but as long as they spell your name correctly, my advice is not to fret about the fashion report.

Colors

In the animal kingdom, it is the male who gets the plumage and splendid colors. In the business world, women get the chance. Whereas men are confined to dark suits and white shirts, women have a broad spectrum of colors from which to choose. Even in countries where it is advisable to dress

Appearance matters.

conservatively (see the Country Profiles), you need not limit yourself to a severely cut navy suit with a white shirt. Wear something which makes you feel good and adds a touch of color to the business world.

Style

Of course, you don't want what you are wearing to speak louder than you do. For the business world, clothes need to be tasteful and tailored.

In most countries, men's alterations are made without charge. Women usually have to pay extra, but it is worth the added cost to have clothes that fit properly.

Watch out for wrinkles. Not laugh lines, but the ones that materialize when you stand up. It helps to test an outfit for "lap wrinkles" before you buy it by sitting down in the dressing room. Another trick is to take a handful of fabric and crush it in your hand. If it wrinkles, don't buy. Lightweight wool crepe doesn't wrinkle and is suitable in most climates. If you do buy something new, break it in first.

Skirts or Trousers?

With few exceptions, trousers are fine. Acceptable lengths for skirts vary from country to country, so check the Country Profiles.

> When I asked a French client what she would wear when she spoke at a conference, she replied with a canny smile, "I shall wear a short skirt because I have good looking legs. Once I have everyone's attention, I will give my message." Typically Parisian, n'est-ce pas? She understood her audience and made her decision accordingly.
>
> On the other side of the globe, Yuri Lustenberger-Kim counsels, "When you are speaking in Korea, a pleated skirt works well, and it must come below your knees." (Check Country Profile pages.)

Jewelry

Keep it simple. Avoid earrings that flash and dangle or bracelets that jangle. You don't want anything to distract from your message.

Rings? According to body language expert Samy Molcho, if you wear a ring on a finger other than the "ring finger" (your third finger), you are sending a signal. Women who wear a ring on their baby finger (some call it a "pinkie ring") are outgoing and social creatures. A woman who wears a ring on the middle finger is short on self-confidence and is seeking self-esteem. A woman who wears a ring on her index finger is a "know it all." If you start observing, you may choose to agree or disagree with these findings. Choosing to wear lots of rings or none at all may also be significant.

Shoes and Stockings

Let's hear it for heels. I wear shoes with heels when I am giving a speech so that the audience can see me better, and I can see my audience better, too. Two and one-half inches does make a difference. (I carry them along just for the event because otherwise I prefer low-heeled shoes.)

You will hardly ever go wrong if you wear neutral colored stockings (tights, pantyhose, whatever you call them.) In some cultures bare legs are unacceptable. Be sure to bring along an extra pair of tights. (In my briefcase, I always carry an extra pair in a discreet envelope; the same for other emergency products.)

Look Your Best

Look your best. If that involves a trip to the hairdresser, think of it as a business expense. Choose a hairstyle which suits you and doesn't require constant fiddling. Keep your hair away from your face so your audience can see your eyes.

If you wear glasses, invest in frames which flatter your face and coloring. I've never understood the woman who spends money on clothes and skimps on glasses which she wears day after day. As eyes are the most expressive part of our face, you might want to consider contact lenses.

If you don't normally wear make-up, I urge you make an exception when you are giving a speech. Your audience spends lot of time looking at your face. A glow on your lips and cheeks makes a positive difference and adds another touch of color to the bland business world.

If you blush easily, you need to control everything that might start that embarrassing red flush from traveling up your neck into your face. Being well-prepared and rehearsed is the best antidote. The more experience you gain, the easier it gets. (They didn't call her the "blushing bride" for nothing.)

If you feel the flushing start, acknowledge it by saying, "When I get involved in what I am saying, sometimes my face gets red, but I don't let it stop me." A suit or blouse in a rich warm color can serve as "camouflage." Make-up foundation, which is a darker shade than your own skin tone, will also help.

Hands are expressive and are invaluable in supporting your words. Keep them well-groomed. Whether or not to wear nail polish should be dictated by your preference, but for the record, the most vociferous complaints I hear against "red nails" are lodged by both men and women who find them unprofessional.

Make It Happen!

Once you have accepted the challenge of raising your voice, you need an opportunity. You might even have to finagle an invitation. Be prepared for any exigency.

> Let's say it is your boss who has been invited. He says, "I don't have the time to travel all the way to Cape Town just to give a speech."
>
> Position yourself. Say, "That's understandable, but it's an honor that you were invited. The top companies in our sector will be there, and we ought to be represented. Not only does this conference give us a unique chance to showcase our achievements, but also we could get some valuable press coverage. What about sending someone else, someone who is up to speed on our latest projects and would take the time to prepare a really power-packed message that the delegates wouldn't forget."
>
> When he asks blankly, "Who are you thinking of?" don't cave in and sigh, "Oh, forget it." Hold your head high and say confidently, "My presentation last month got positive feedback from the entire staff. I think that you should send me in your place." If he is hesitant, continue, "You know we have a real campaign to promote women in the public eye. So far the list of confirmed speakers for this conference doesn't include one woman. They would like to have a woman speaker, and it would make us look good, too. If you recommend me, the organizers will surely agree."

I hope you heard the assurance in that woman's voice. I hope you took note of her strong reasons. I hope you felt her poise.

Take Center Stage!

What if you are given a choice between giving a presentation or taking part in a panel discussion? The prospect of not being alone on the stage sounds appealing, doesn't it? You won't feel so exposed. Consider it carefully.

As soon as you have to share the stage, you may run into the same difficulties that often plague women in the boardroom or the classroom where you are ignored or interrupted. If you are less aggressive than your male counterparts, you appear meek and self-effacing. If you demand equal time, you may be perceived as a bulldozer.

When you do serve on a panel, contribute at the very beginning to signal that you will be actively involved and not merely a passive member. The first time you are interrupted, say in a cool strong voice, "Wait. I am talking." Do not ask permission to continue as in, "May I please finish?" If you are interrupted again, you can put out your hand as you say, "Stop. I am not finished." Use short sentences beginning with "I." Keep a pleasant expression on your face.

Now do you see why it's preferable to "go solo"?

Being in the spotlight lets people learn about you and see you in action. These days someone who can communicate competently is a prize possession. You will be taken seriously and increase your value to your employers.

In addition to which, at the majority of conferences today, there is rarely more than one woman speaker. If you are that woman, your organization gets recognition because they have an intelligent and articulate woman to represent them. That's good public relations. And because you are in the minority, the one woman among many men, both you and your firm will be remembered.

Use your new skills in your personal as well as in your professional life. Command attention by raising your voice and by controlling the silence. Focus your words and pronounce them with clarity and precision. Move with poise. You gain immense satisfaction from being able to speak for yourself.

When you are invited to speak at a conference don't say, "Who, me? Oh, I have never done that. I get so nervous."

Instead, say "Yes, I accept with pleasure" and keep reading!

Propose a Toast, Moderate a Conference and Other Speaking Pleasures

In addition to full-fledged business presentations, many other speaking opportunities exist. Always say "yes" to special assignments. In addition to doing a great service for whoever asks you, you will have one more chance to practice the techniques presented in this book.

Proposing a Toast

Giving a toast should be a warm and heartfelt experience not a duty carried out begrudgingly. As usual, knowing what to say in advance helps. In some countries and at some events, a formal ritual must be observed. In other places, the rules are relaxed. Check the Country Profiles to find out which scenario applies at the event you will be attending.

In proposing a toast, follow these general guidelines:

- Be sure there is something to drink in everyone's glass. (It need not be alcohol — juice or water is fine.)

- Rise and get the audience's attention. Instead of tapping a piece of cutlery against a glass which may result in shattered crystal, clink two glasses together at the widest part of the glass (which is also the strongest part). The resulting sound is melodious and resounding! If this is a grand event and musicians are present as part of the entertainment, ask if they will give you a musical fanfare.

- Then you may want to hold one glass high in the air to signal you are going to make a toast, but put it down while you are speaking.

🥂 If necessary, prepare speaker's notes with the proper order of names, titles and correct pronunciations. If you write large enough, you can place the card on the table for easy reference.

🥂 Direct your first words to the person or group you are honoring. Thereafter include all guests in your gaze.

🥂 Be brief.

🥂 Conclude by letting the audience know exactly what they are to do: "Please stand and raise your glasses to the Rising Sun Enterprises and Chairman Kim for arranging this splendid symposium."

🥂 The person being toasted remains seated and nods in appreciation.

🥂 Remember, the best toast is like champagne — uplifting and effervescent.

Responding to a Toast

If you are the honored guest who has just been toasted, it is customary to return the toast. Ideally, you should respond immediately. The longer you wait the more agonizing it becomes. Simply rise and say, "Thank you, Jeff, for your kind toast. May I express my appreciation to you and the Greenfield Summit for making this event possible. Participating in this

Be uplifting and effervescent.

forum has been a privilege and a pleasure. I am sure everyone joins me in saying 'thank you.'" Then you raise your glass and everyone (except Jeff) follows suit.

Moderating a Conference

You may have been chosen to moderate a conference because of your communication skills, or it may be your responsibility because you are the president of the host organization. As with all speaking situations, the more you know about your surroundings and the better prepared you are, the more smoothly the experience will go.

When you moderate a conference, your model should be the swan: elegant and unruffled on the surface and paddling like hell underneath. With what appears to be effortless ease, you strive to keep everyone on time, moving in the right direction, and in an upbeat mood while handling disasters with the speed of a bicycle courier, the mechanical skills of a fix-it man and the finesse of a diplomat.

Before the Conference

You need to meet with the person in charge of the conference center or hotel to check out the facilities. Even assuming that your responsibilities do not include organizing the coffee breaks and buffet lunches, it still helps to be completely familiar with the layout of the conference center. You may need to reach the interpreters' booths or the slide projection room in a hurry. (In Amsterdam, I needed to consult with the slide projectionist about strange markings which suddenly appeared on the slides during the first speaker's presentation. The fastest route was behind the scenes: through the serving kitchen and up a flight of stairs.)

When you make an appointment to see the conference room, specify that you want to actually get inside the room. If you take the time to have a preliminary look around, you do not want to discover that another conference is in progress and all you can do is look through a peep hole or wait until the group adjourns for dinner.

If possible, meet the staff who will actually be on duty the day of your conference. If you know their names and functions, you will be able to say, "Miss Chlepnac, would you please locate another spotlight for the left side of the stage? By the way, the flowers are lovely." Know which equipment will be used for your conference. Ask to check it out in advance. If something goes wrong, the audience will probably expect you to handle the situation. You don't want to appear unprofessional.

Preserve Your Sanity: Carry a Clipboard

Do not underestimate the value of a clipboard. Guard it with your life. If your name is prominently displayed and you misplace it, it will be returned. (No one else wants your responsibilities.)

In addition to the actual schedule, you need the names and pager numbers of conference staff as well as complete information about the speakers. That includes their speech titles and your introductory remarks. Be sure all names are written out correctly, phonetically if necessary. If titles are used, double-check for accuracy. Know how to reach all the speakers. If you are staying at a conference hotel, include their room extension numbers so that you can keep track of them.

Schedule a "Dry Run" Rehearsal for the Day Before

It helps to have a dress rehearsal with all the speakers. Ideally, they should arrive early enough to give their entire speech standing in the right spot, practicing with the microphone and checking out the slides. (For some, it may be the first time they run through their entire presentation.) If time is limited, at least have them stand on the stage and practice the beginning and end of their talks using the microphone. At a conference which I coordinated in Budapest, we discovered the speakers were unable to see their slides when they were at the lectern. Early the following morning, we were able to have a platform installed which allowed the speakers to see their slides and be seen by their audience.

Start and Finish on Time

For their first conference in Warsaw, Dow Europe arbitrarily set a 9 a.m. starting time. When they learned that participants would be traveling from great distances, they rescheduled the conference for 11 a.m. and served coffee beforehand. When you begin, you don't want your audience stuck in a traffic jam.

Once you have a convenient starting time, enforce it. No one minds beginning a little late, but everyone dislikes running over time. Unfortunately, people forget that the two are related.

Get the Conference Off to a Strong Start

As the moderator, you are instrumental in establishing the mood for the entire conference. Your first words need to be lively and positive to get the conference off to a great start. Delay the housekeeping matters, such as lavatory locations and smoking regulations, until later in the program. However, if simultaneous interpretation is provided, begin by explaining how to use the headphones. Holding a set, say, "We don't want you to miss a single word. Our interpreters are ready to go! *Pour entendre en français numéro un, für Deutsch auf zwei.*"

It helps to be aware of the psychology of headphones. Many participants avoid using them. They listen to the speaker in her original language to practice their language skills. They may not want other delegates to be aware they are not fluent in the speaker's language. However, when they start losing the thread, they reach for the headphones. By now the speaker is well into her talk. It is disconcerting for her to watch her audience fumble around in order to get the right channel.

Remind your audience to switch off their mobile phones (cellular phones, handys, Natels dependent upon the country.) Simply hold up a phone and smile broadly as you speak into it saying, "Sorry, I'm going to switch off my phone right now. I'm at a great conference and do not want to disturb anyone." You may need to remind people again after coffee or lunch breaks.

Introduce the Speakers

Finally, it is time to introduce the first speaker. To give winning introductions, please refer to the "Introducing Another Speaker" section later in this chapter.

Sit in a Convenient Spot

Where should you sit? Preferably not on the stage. When you are in full view of the audience, it inhibits your being able to leave or receive messages discreetly. Try to sit in the first row, on an aisle and near an exit. From this vantage point, you can signal to the speaker, if need be. You can see what's happening on the screen, and with a turn of your head, you can keep an eye on the audience, too.

When I moderate a conference, I have coached the speakers in advance so they are familiar with my system of signals. Seated at the side in the front row (or if need be at the very back of the room), I cue the speakers with color-coded time cards: green = 5 minutes, yellow = 2 minutes, orange = 1 minute. The red sign says STOP! If they want me to, I also flash cards which say, "slow down" or "smile" or even "breathe." (I hold these cards discreetly, so only the speakers are aware of them.)

Ask your staff to keep messages to the minimum. Have them written out which is less disconcerting than whispering in your ear. ("Tell Dr. Hanson that her patient has just gone into labor," or "Inform the owner of the green Saab that his car is being towed.")

What if Speakers Run Overtime?

You may need to stand up and say, "You need to finish in 30 seconds so that our planned program can be maintained." Thirty seconds is enough time for any speaker to conclude. If you give him more time, he may abuse it.

Obviously, whether or not you interfere depends upon the speaker's status. You won't interrupt your prime minister!

> I moderated a gala dinner where 22 people were invited to speak. Each speaker received a letter which said: "You have been invited to say 'a few words.' Because our program is power-packed, we ask you to limit yourself to three minutes. From experience, three minutes is about 400 words. Whether you use a script or speak extemporaneously, please time your talk in advance so we can get the speeches, the entertainment and the meal completed before midnight. We appreciate your brevity!" The experienced speakers adhered to the time limit while the less experienced speakers began by saying "Three minutes is too short to say anything" and then proved it.

How Do You Get People Back from the Break?

Most moderators announce, "We will reconvene in 20 minutes." If you ask the delegates to be back in 18 minutes, you make them slightly more aware of the elapsing time. To enforce the time, I start my stopwatch when the break begins. Then, with five minutes left, I approach the people at the far corner the refreshment area and say, "Will you help me get everyone back into the room. We want to start on time so we can end on time!" Then I smile and wait until they start moving. A firm but friendly approach works well.

(For dealing with Question and Answer sessions and other potentially difficult situations with ease, please refer to Chapter 8.)

Finish with Flair

As the conference moderator, you need to provide a running commentary which links one speaker to the other and gives the audience a thoughtful framework. At the end of the conference, a final summary is in order. Ideally you will energetically sum up each speaker's contribution and add a final message of your own. The ending of your conference needs to be strong and dynamic, just like the ending of an individual speech. And you want to end on time while the delegates are still in the audience and not on their way to the airport.

Introducing Another Speaker

Like a preview of coming attractions at the cinema, a winning introduction lets the audience know they are in for something special. Regrettably, good introductions are few and far between. At many conferences, someone just reads off a "laundry list" of degrees and achievements, often from the program notes which the audience has in front of them. At other times, the moderator gets carried away and delivers a full-fledged speech of his own.

Don't underestimate how much impact a few well-chosen and expertly delivered words can have on the speaker as well. By the time you have finished, she should be eager to speak.

If you learn my "WIN" by heart, you can use it on a spur of the moment.

If you know the speaker personally, include a few words about how you met or time you have spent together. But keep the focus on your speaker. However, while you are making the introduction, resist the universal temptation to look at the speaker. She knows who she is. Direct your words to your audience. This gives the speaker one last chance to compose herself before she is in the limelight. Although the speaker you are introducing is rarely a mystery, it adds a soupçon of surprise to hold off mentioning her name until the very end. Besides, it fulfills my definition of a good conclusion: save the best for last.

Remember to pronounce her name correctly. The best way is to practice in advance.

Here is an introduction which got the speaker off to a flying start!

We are delighted that our next speaker has arrived from the United States to share with us the developments that she has masterminded

---

How to Give a Winning Introduction?

W: Explain *why* this particular speaker is addressing this audience today.

I: *Intrigue* the audience with a specific fact or question to get them sitting on the edges of their seats, curious and attentive.

N: Announce the speaker's *name* at the end of your introduction. Only now should the focus switch from you to the speaker.

Be brief! Limit yourself to one to two minutes. When possible, ask the speaker in advance what to include. Avoid "laundry lists" of the speaker's degrees, jobs, etc.

If appropriate (and it usually is), ask the audience to "give a warm welcome to Ms Stella Steelface." Then generate some applause to accompany the speaker as she/he strides forward.

After you help the speaker adjust the mike, check for a glass of water, etc., you should fade into the shadows but stand guard during the talk to deal with any disasters that might crop up.

How to Get a Winning Introduction?

Make sure the person introducing you knows these guidelines.

---

and overseen. So far, on this side of the Atlantic, we have not had the chance to even glimpse what this product can do. We have only heard rumors of how good it is. Today these rumors will be verified once and for all! Occasionally you may hear that our speaker has her head in the clouds, but I can assure you that is only when she is piloting her own single-engine airplane across the country. Let's give a warm welcome to Global Business and R & D Director of Dow: Nancy Morris.

Of course, when you are the speaker you also deserve a winning introduction! The easiest way is to compose your own and send it in advance to the person who will be introducing you. It is a good idea to title it: "Suggested Introductory Remarks for My Talk." If you say "suggested," you will not insult your host who may have already penned some winning words. When I propose this to my clients, they often think it a bit immodest. You may feel the same, but wouldn't you be pleased to get special information if you were doing the introductions? Not surprisingly, such prepared introductory remarks are always used, possibly not verbatim. Since you have taken the time to write your own introduction, take along a copy in case another person ends up introducing you.

Introducing Yourself

Two typical scenarios: You are seated at a boardroom table with a dozen other managers. Or you are striding to the front of a hotel ballroom to deliver a speech. Suddenly whoever is in charge blithely says, "Why don't you introduce yourself."

How do you react? Most of us panic. Why? Because we hate talking about ourselves and don't want to be accused of blatant self-promotion. And because we are unprepared.

How not to do it: A senior manager traveled to Germany to facilitate a three-day meeting. His introduction was so brief that everyone wondered, "Why has he come?" Had he mentioned his international experience and qualifications, his audience would have thought, "We are so glad he is here!"

How to do it: Ed Roberts, newly-arrived Head of Discovery Chemistry at Roche was invited to address the prestigious Chemical Society of Basel at a formal luncheon. He assumed that the society's chairman would introduce him. I urged Ed to create his own introduction, and Ed agreed it was a wise precaution.

During our session, and following the usual formula, Ed began with his name and title. Then he listed his degrees, patents and academic connections. Very impressive! As we watched the videotape of this dry-run, Ed spontaneously said, "Whatever took me so long to come to Basel? It is the world-wide center of excellence for chemistry." What a great first sentence that would make! In fact, when the Swiss chairman did ask Ed if he wouldn't mind introducing himself, Ed began with that very sentence. He created "instant rapport" and made each member of the Chemical Society feel proud and special.

Why not create your own introduction? Right now. Take paper and pen or turn on your laptop. Then the next time, you will be ready!

Start with a simple statement or question. Avoid beginning with the words "My name is . . ." or "I." (Why? You need to give your brain a jolt.)

Be specific. Instead of "I work for a large international organization" say "Seventeen countries, 11 languages, 7 time zones. That is my challenge as the Director of HR Europe for Sulzer. And I love it. My name is Astrid Sterchi."

Share your goals and dreams. Instead of, "I am an educator" say "My goal is to make a profound contribution to the education of gifted and talented children. My name is Robin Kyburg."

Begin with the unexpected. "Stagnation is not my idea of a good time. That is why I love the reinsurance business. My name is Dirk Lohmann. I'm the CEO of Converium."

Take a light-hearted approach. "An auditor explaining how to improve government performance can put an audience to sleep in ten minutes, a good one can do it in four. My name is Erik Peters; I am the Auditor General of Ontario."

Since my move to Chicago, I have updated my own introduction. Now I say,

"Speaking is what I do. I train clients worldwide to speak effectively. Speaking Globally is my book. When I speak, it is about speaking. My name is Beth Urech and my company is Speaking Unlimited."

Once the framework is solid, you can add or subtract to suit each occasion. Your introduction can be low-key or power-packed. In the event that you are not fully introduced the way you should be, you can forge your own connection to your audience. Whatever happens, you will be prepared.

Now, would you please introduce yourself . . .

The Elevator Speech

Currently popular with MBA and Executive Education programs, the elevator speech sets up the following scenario:

You walk across the lobby of a building and enter an elevator. Just as the doors start to shut, in walks the CEO you want to work with or the HR Director of the firm you hope to join. Maybe it's the man or woman of your dreams.

You have thirty floors, approximately thirty seconds, in which to explain why you, your product, your vision, goals and/or dreams are unique and indispensable to your "captured" audience. Every word, gesture and pause is at a premium because when the doors open on the 30th floor your time is up.

You can say a lot in thirty seconds if you are prepared.

Here's one of my elevator speeches, and it almost happened this way!

"Good morning, Mr. Lohmann. Hail to the victors valiant!"

He's caught bit off-guard, but I've done my homework and know Dirk Lohmann who is a German citizen graduated from The University of Michigan as did I. So a line from the fight song will hopefully break the ice. He smiles. It has worked.

"Yes," I continue. "I went to Michigan, too. Great school, isn't it?" He nods.

"Your HR director suggested you and I meet. As you can hear, I'm an American. However, I help European executives like you sharpen your speaking skills."

He's non-committal.

"I work with video. You see yourself the way others do. First we assess your strong points, then target what to improve. You see the results immediately. I know you have a major speech next month. What better time to get started."

Elevator opens.

"Talk to Jana, my assistant," says Mr. Lohmann as he strides away. "Set up a session."

Create your own Elevator Speech. Practice with a friend or colleague in an elevator or even better on videotape. Find an opening ice-breaker. Say what you do and how you can help. Don't wait to be asked. Be sure to include why you are the right person for the job.

Of course, you need to tailor your message to the person and his alma mater or her organization.

Once you get your thirty-second pitch in place, a hall-talk (five minutes) or a seated-next-to-on-the airplane opportunity will be a breeze.

Now jump on the elevator and take it to the top.

Accepting an Award with TACT

If you know in advance you are receiving an award or recognition, you have time to compose a few words of gratitude. However, if the occasion comes as a surprise, you need not be left speechless. Just accept with TACT! First, stride to the front of the room. When you reach the person who is giving you the award, shake hands, kiss on both cheeks, whatever is appropriate. Then take the award graciously.

Now you will be expected to say a few words. If you have not had the opportunity to compose some clever or touching words in advance, let the award be your starting point. Describe where you will display the trophy, when you will drink the wine or how you will use the money. If you get a gift-wrapped box, you probably will not want to take the time to open it. Besides which, in some countries, such as Korea, it is inappropriate to open a gift when you receive it. "Thank you for your thoughtfulness" will suffice.

Although you may be inclined to talk exclusively to the person who is doing the honors, it is more cordial to acknowledge the other people in the room by turning and including them: "I am glad you are here to share in this wonderful moment." If they have contributed to your success, say so. "You have helped me earn this. Without your hard work, we never could have raised the money to build a children's wing on the hospital."

Your actual words are not as important as your attitude. That is what your audience will remember. Then, to use an old Woody Allen phrase, "Take the money and run," which is another way of saying that you don't want to turn this into a major production. Smile and say "thank you" as you return to your seat.

So, now you know how to accept an award with TACT:

Thank the person giving you the award.

Acknowledge your audience.

Comment on the award.

Take the money and run!

CHAPTER

12

Face the Media without Losing Face

As business executives around the world have learned to their chagrin, the only thing that's off the record is what you don't say. This chapter gives you guidelines on how to handle a typical "Breakfast Business News" interview as well as pointers for a crisis scenario.

For many business executives, a TV appearance is one of the rare occasions when you are not calling the shots. You have to accept this reversal of power. In a media interview, you are not in control. You are in a no-win situation. You have to avoid getting frustrated or furious. Keep in mind how childish this would appear to the at-home audience. Act accordingly.

Although it often appears that the media is out to get you, what journalists are really after is a good story — unfortunately this normally means action, conflict, drama and disaster. If you are totally prepared for a lively and concise exchange of words and can supply urgency and energy about your area of expertise, you may satisfy their minimum daily requirements. Who knows, you may get invited back. It pays to know the rules.

> ❧ Rule number 1: Journalists make the rules.

> ❧ Rule number 2: You need to learn the rules.

> ❧ Rule number 3: If you break the rules, you will be the loser.

Pros and Cons of Television Interviews

With the odds against you, why in the world would you ever agree to a TV interview? Because it is great exposure for you and your firm. A two-minute interview in the business slot of the morning broadcast reaches thousands of viewers. A 10-second "sound bite" on the night time news may reach millions of listeners. And it is free coverage.

If you decide it is in the best interests of you and your organization to give an interview, then you need to prepare thoroughly. You will also have to allocate several hours, most of which will be spent waiting either at the studio or in a conference center hospitality lounge — wherever the interview is scheduled to take place. "Lights, camera, action!" may be the cue, but hours of setting up the lights and camera are required before there is any action!

Before Your Interview

Watch the program in advance to familiarize yourself with the format and the interviewer's style. If that isn't possible, ask the producer to send you a sample videotape of the show or ask a local colleague to give you a briefing. In Europe, most business formats are straightforward; however some interviewers are heavy-handed. In Asia, you can usually expect fair treatment. In the USA, find out if the format is straight news or "info-tainment." (The term combines "information" and "entertainment" with the emphasis on the entertainment aspect. These programs take a slick and superficial angle to serious and not-so-serious issues. Unless you have great flair and presence, you may be overwhelmed.)

Always keep in mind that your real audience is the one at home. The interviewer is merely the conduit through whom you are speaking. Sometimes even seasoned television guests forget this. If they get an unfair question, they get cantankerous and may even explode. Remember television is a "cool" medium. "Calm and collected" are the operative words. Emotional outbursts look unprofessional and should be avoided.

Prepare Your Key Points

After you find out why you have been asked for an interview and what slant the interviewer plans to take, determine what you want to accomplish. Are you introducing a new concept or product? Are you reinforcing an existing policy? Are you defending yourself and your organization against spurious attacks or calming the public's fears? If you and your interviewer have different agendas, you may have to work hard to get your message across, but you can do it if you try. Practice stating your key points in less than ten words, and then memorize them. For example: "We're the first truly pan-European telecom company" or "China needs the world, and the world needs China."

Since interviews are normally two minutes or less, two or three key points are all you will need. Probably one of them should be the name of your firm. Use it as often as you can. Instead of saying "we" or "I," say, "At Speaking Unlimited . . ."

Practice the Q → A + 1 Formula

When you get a question which could be answered with "yes" or "no," use my Q → A + 1 formula. Instead of responding with a one-word answer, add a "positive plus point" to keep the conversation moving. If you are asked, "Are you expanding in China?" answer, "Yes. We plan to expand our sales outlets in seven major Chinese cities in the coming year."

Anticipate Difficult Questions

Anticipate all the questions you will be asked. Then formulate your answers. Practice your answers out loud. As I have said elsewhere in *Speaking Globally*, you have to be able to get your mouth around the words. One client who was concerned about being caught off-guard wrote down the answers to 80 potential questions and practiced them out loud. He was asked only five questions and was so cool and collected that he looked more professional than his interviewer.

What are the most difficult questions you could be asked about your personal life, your credentials, your business or your clients? What is the one question you do not ever want to answer about your personal life, your credentials, your business or your clients? Don't wait until you are in the studio or a reporter is at your front door shoving a microphone in your face to figure out a suitable answer.

Sensitive questions usually concern sex, politics and religion. I would add money. Especially salaries. If you are asked what you earned last year, you have several options. You can tell the truth, you can lie, you can say "no comment" or you can answer the question tactfully without revealing anything. If you say, "I earned $2 million," don't be surprised if you are asked, "How can you justify your exorbitant salary when your company just laid off 800 people?"

Prevarication can get you into trouble. Journalists have their sources for uncovering the truth. Even a friend or colleague might offer to set the record straight. There's something to be said for the old adage: "Never tell your best friend something you wouldn't want your worst enemy to hear."

Never say "No comment." Those words will immediately condemn you. Journalists and the public at home will assume that you are trying to hide something. If you cannot answer because of company policy or proprietary rights, frame your answer carefully. Here is a suggestion: "Our company policy has determined that this information remains private." If the interviewer persists, continue, "As a journalist, you certainly want to get the facts, but in this case that isn't possible." Don't add a qualifier like, "I wish it were." When you are finished, stop talking.

"So at the risk of being persistent, how much did you earn last year?" "I am not going to tell you how much I earned last year, but it was enough to pay the bills and to put some away so that I will be able to watch your show when I am retired." Or: "That amount is off the record, but it is more than I thought I would be able to make when I started my firm ten years ago. That just goes to show how hard work and determination can still succeed in today's rapidly changing world."

In both cases, you have said nothing but you have not lost face and neither has your interviewer! Usually, the more succinct your answer, the better it comes across. Set up a private practice session in advance of meeting the interviewer. Complete the fact sheet (Figure 12.1) in advance.

Dress Conservatively

What you wear on television is important. Dress conservatively and choose medium shades in the color spectrum. Gray, dark blue and jewel tones look good on camera. However, don't blend in with the background. If you know you will be seated on a blue sofa, don't wear blue. Avoid pure white, shiny fabrics and busy patterns. Don't wear photosensitive glasses which react to light because as soon as the studio lights are on, your lenses will darken, turning you into a Mafia gang leader.

Special tips for women: Flashy jewelry and dangling earrings are distracting, as are skirts that ride up. Be sure that your skirt is long and comfortable. You

FIGURE 12.1 Fact sheet for interviews

Fact Sheet for Interviews

Date: _____ Time: _____ Length: _____

Show: _____ ❏ Radio ❏ TV

Format: _____ ❏ Live ❏ Taped

Host/hostess's name: _____

Topic: _____

Your three-point agenda: _____

   1. _____

   2. _____

   3. _____

Target audience: _____

Editing rights: _____ Can you record segment: _____

Notes/requests: _____

_____

Contact's name: _____

Producer's and director's name: _____

Names of technicians and crew: _____

_____

Studio address: _____

Studio telephone: _____ Fax: _____

Evaluation: _____

Thank you: _____

don't want to fiddle with it when you are seated. In some countries, short sleeves and trousers are taboo, so check the Country Profiles in advance.

Special tips for men: Wear over-the-calf socks. Exposing bare leg is tacky. Your socks should match the color of your shoes which should be black or dark brown. If you perspire profusely, pack an extra shirt in your briefcase. If you have a heavy beard, shave just before you arrive or make arrangements to shave in the studio dressing room.

AVOID GLASSES
WHICH DARKEN

→ LOOK AT INTERVIEWER →

HANDS QUIET

DON'T SWIVEL!

LONG SOCKS, PLEASE

See yourself as the viewer does.

At the Studio

Television studios are often messy and tasteless. The leather-bound books are fake; the carpet has cigarette holes in it. The plants and flowers are plastic. Besides which, the coffee is horrible. Don't let any of this bother you. Welcome to the world of illusion. Plan to arrive early and include enough time to get lost en route. Television studios are rarely in the best part of town so it may take longer than you think to find the address or a parking place.

Make-Up

You will probably be ushered into the studio and asked to wait. You may be taken to the make-up department. If you are a woman and have already done your make-up, it may suffice. Otherwise get ready for a makeover. If you are a man, accept wearing make-up. (Be prepared for touch-ups with powder in the studio. By the way, if the make-up person spills loose powder all over your dark jacket, she may be following instructions from the producer who wants to get you upset. It is juvenile, but it often works.)

Familiarize Yourself with the Surroundings

Once you are in the studio, familiarize yourself with the cameras, the monitors, the microphones and the lights. Sit down where you will be seated. Sit well back in the chair and then lean forward slightly from the waist to convey a sense of interest and urgency. If sofas or oversized arm chairs are provided, don't cross your legs and get too comfortable. To your viewers, you will look arrogant. If you are placed in a swivel chair, practice not swiveling or you will look nervous.

If you are lucky, the producer, assistant producer or interviewer will arrive and run through the program's format with you. You may even be told which questions you will be asked, but don't count on it. Interviewers are notoriously fickle, and if they sniff a controversy brewing, they may change the script as soon as the show is under way.

Make a point of learning everyone's name. It helps to warm up the atmosphere and will be appreciated by the crew who are often referred to as "Hey, you."

Establish Ground Rules

You need to establish ground rules before the "on the air" sign flashes. If some issues are off limits, make that clear beforehand. For example, you can say, "I am willing to discuss the closing of our local plant and how this will affect employees, however, I am unable to give you the details of our proposed merger. Do you agree?" At this point, the interviewer and the producer will agree. They are fully aware that they cannot do the interview without you.

In the course of the interview, if you are asked about the merger, look at the interviewer with feigned amazement and say slowly, "We agreed beforehand not to discuss this." If your interviewer persists (he or she probably will), shake your head quizzically and reiterate, "We agreed earlier not to discuss this issue." Then stop speaking. Your audience will get the message.

When I worked in television, I once interviewed the newly-appointed first woman vice-president of a major bank. She was nervous and asked if we could have a dress rehearsal. For 15 minutes, we had a witty warm-up session. However, the actual interview was uninspired and tedious because we had used up our energy in the rehearsal. I never made that mistake again.

Check Yourself on the Monitor

You should ask to see yourself in the monitor before the cameras start running. You have a right to know if you have a piece of spinach caught in your teeth, or worse. Several years ago, a major television network interviewed a prominent banker whose bulging shirt exposed his protruding belly. I am sure the television crew noticed this *faux pas*, but no one suggested he button his jacket or sit behind a desk because his bare skin made good television. Pull down your jacket so that it doesn't bunch up around your neck. Once you have checked your appearance, then forget the monitor completely.

Sit straight, lean forward. While you are being introduced, you should convey authority, warmth and confidence. The look on your face should say, "I know something that you don't know . . . but don't go away and you will soon find out."

During the Interview

Establish immediate eye contact with your interviewer. From now on, ignore the camera, the monitor and all studio distractions. Don't rely on the red light on the camera to accurately signal whether you are on camera or not. Stories attest to cameras being falsely hooked up. Even when you are not speaking, you may be on camera. You cannot predict when the director will call for a "reaction shot," which may find you blowing your nose, or worse.

You may not actually be in the same studio with your interviewer; for example, she is in New York and you are in a studio in Bombay. In this case, convention dictates that you look directly at your camera as if you could see her through the lens. If you are given a tiny earpiece to put into your ear, it will drive you crazy. It's called an IFB (interrupt feedback). This is part of the process so don't complain. Just make the most of it and remember that your advertising budget can't afford this kind of coverage.

If the interviewer plies you with "yes and no" questions, remember my Q → A + 1 formula. Answer the question and then add a positive comment. For example, if you are asked, "Are you selling online?" you can answer, "yes" or "no." Or you can use the Q → A + 1 formula and say, "Yes, and it's especially useful to reach our clients in Asia." Use signal words like "What's important is . . ." and "I want to underline . . .".

Although the majority of questions will be straightforward, you should be prepared for tricky questions. If you listen carefully, you probably will not be caught off-guard. Beware of leading questions and loaded questions! A leading question is one in which your expected answer is implied. Your interviewer says, "You do agree that we have to separate human rights' issues from trade policy, don't you?" If you agree, say so, and move on. If you do not agree, avoid beginning with, "No" or "I disagree." Phrase your answer in positive terms. A loaded question involves an accusation: "Are you still exaggerating the number of your on-time flights?" Don't fall for this trap by answering "no," and don't repeat the word "exaggerating." Say, "Our on-time record is one of the best in the industry."

Do not be afraid of silence. Sometimes an interviewer will hesitate after you have given your answer in the hope that you will continue talking out of courtesy and unwittingly reveal something you didn't intend to say. Avoid the urge to fill the silence. If your interviewer doesn't break in, you could ask innocently, "What else would you like to ask me?" But why bother? "Dead air" is your interviewer's problem, not yours!

When you don't know the answer, glance down naturally while you are figuring out what to say. If you look up, you signal total ignorance. Check yourself out on a video camera, and you will see what I mean. Gesturing is fine, but do keep your hands away from your face since you won't be able to gauge whether the camera has you in a head shot, a shoulder shot or a waist shot. For the same reason, avoid quick, jerky movements.

Once you feel comfortable on camera, you may want to try to bend the rules a little by bridging from your interviewer's questions to your agenda, but beware. Politicians have become so adept at this technique that it has become suspect. After all, how do you react if someone smoothly says, "You'd like to know about our record of environmental clean up. Let me just say that our profits rose 8 per cent last month."

When the questioning gets hot and heavy, stay cool and slow down. Journalists thrive on conflict and controversy. If they get you stirred up, they may get a pay bonus. If you are unable to contain your emotions, then do not attack your interviewer. Attack the issues involved. "Yes, I am upset — in fact I am furious — at the lack of controls on child labor."

If your interview is more than five minutes long, do not hesitate to repeat your key point. That is why you have learned variations on a theme! Strive to be clear, concise and quotable.

On-location interviews can be difficult.

Once again, remember that the only thing that is "off the record" is what you don't say. Even if you are told that the cameras are no longer running, an open microphone can be recording your comments.

On-Location Interviews

Nowadays, video equipment is so portable that interviewers may prefer to meet you at your hotel. Reserve a conference room or locate a secluded corner where the distractions will not overwhelm you. TV crews are impervious to disasters which do not concern them, but you may not be immune to passers-by gaping at you while you try to conduct a scintillating interview in the busy lobby.

If you agree to an interview in your office, expect cables, bright lights and total confusion which will throw your staff into a panic mode. If you decide to use a vacant office to alleviate these inconveniences, the audience will sense that you are not in your own office.

Live or Taped?

Your initial inclination may be to ask if your interview can be taped in advance of transmission. That way if you make a "blooper" (a silly mistake), you can start over again. Although a taped interview may sound appealing, I advise my clients to "go live." A taped session can be postponed, rescheduled and then canceled. It can also be edited.

Imagine that in a taped interview you say, "I would not agree that I made a miscalculation in negotiating the contracts with our Finnish subsidiary." The editor chops off the first five words, and 10 million listeners hear, "I made a miscalculation in negotiating the contracts with our Finnish subsidiary." It's unethical, and you can sue. You can also avoid such problems by insisting on a live interview.

If you are scheduled for a live slot on Breakfast Business News, you know that you will be on at 8:15 and out of the studio shortly thereafter, unless the show is pre-empted by a disaster. Of course when you are live, the director cannot yell, "Cut," and restart the taping, so if you make a mistake, let it pass or correct yourself, just like you do in real life. The added "buzz" of a live performance provides a good energy level for you, the interviewer and the home audience.

How about alcohol? The lights in a studio are incredibly strong and intensify the effect of alcohol in a big way. The last thing you need is to look intoxicated on the air. If you are a guest on a show where alcohol is served, ask politely for plain water. When the show is over, you can head for the bar.

Editing and broadcasting rights? These legalities need to be investigated by your legal staff. If you are well-prepared, you have little to worry about.

After the Interview

Send a thank you note to the producer and interviewer. The next time you plan to be in town, give them some advance notice and maybe you will get another invitation. Remember, when you do a good job on television, the pay-off is fantastic.

Crisis Interviews

Hopefully you will never be called upon to conduct an interview under duress. However, when a tragedy strikes your firm, the news media can track you down no matter where you are. Here are some guidelines.

Whenever you get a call from a journalist, check her credentials before you agree to an interview. If she insists she needs your answer immediately because of an urgent deadline, ask her to call you back in half an hour. You don't want to face the firing squad until you have adequate ammunition of your own. The same goes for the television crew who appear at your reception area. Let them cool their heels in the lobby until you have done your homework.

Your homework consists of getting the facts. Once you have them, choose clear and concise words to express your reaction to the crisis at hand. What are you already doing to make things better? "We are devastated to learn about the train derailment. As soon as I have more details, I will get back to you. In the meantime, let me say that the entire area is being evacuated."

If there is any suffering involved, you need to address that first.

When I trained the president of a bank, one mock scenario had him disembarking from a flight to be accosted by a journalist who asked, "What do you think about the bomb that killed six employees at your bank's headquarters on Park Avenue?" He immediately replied, "Let me reassure our customers that none of their money has been affected." Heartless man. By the third attempt, he was expressing his deep concern for the families involved. He didn't even mention the money. He had learned that when tragedy strikes, the human side is more important than the financial implications, at least to the viewers at home.

In conclusion, remember that in television interviews, it is the viewers at home who are your audience. You cannot see or hear them, but they can see and hear you intimately. If you approach the television camera with confidence and candor, you will be able to establish rapport with millions of people and remain cool and calm under amazing pressure.

13

Avoid Pitfalls and *Faux Pas*

Once in Germany where I was organizing a conference for General Motors, I requested that the serving staff arrive promptly at five for the after-conference apéro (cocktail hour reception). Imagine my chagrin when the front desk awakened me at dawn and announced, "Guten Morgen! Your waiters have arrived!" Had I followed the European custom and said "Siebzehn Uhr," (seventeen hours), I could have slept later. That's when I adapted to the 24-hour as opposed to the 12-hour format. Just to make doubly-sure, I also add "in the morning" or "in the afternoon."

When you are headed for foreign shores, you may need to reset your vocabulary as well as your watch. As a speaker, you certainly need to tailor your message as well as your wardrobe to each specific audience. In that way, you will be able to stand out on the platform while comfortably fitting in to the local scene.

This chapter includes a selected list of countries around the world with pertinent tips to help you prepare before departure so you know what to expect upon arrival and during your speech. We are living in a fast-forward society where people need to become more aware of cultural differences and try harder to adapt.

These Country Profiles will also help when you are meeting foreign business people in your own country. Of course, sometimes adapting has unforeseen consequences:

When a British banker agreed to discuss pension plan schemes with a Texas organization, its chairman sent out a memo requesting that participants wear dark suits to make a proper impression for their distinguished guest. What a surprise when the banker arrived all decked out in a brand-new Western shirt, string tie and cowboy boots. His desire to adapt to Texas informality delighted his audience. Everyone had a hearty laugh, and his presentation was a rip-roaring success.

The international business world is becoming more "Westernized," though not as Western as the above story might imply!

For example, although traditionally the Chinese and Japanese write their surname first, many now adopt the Western way of putting their given name first, followed by surname. If you are unsure, ask politely. Younger people especially are more readily dropping titles, using first names and dressing more informally.

A concurrent trend is also on the rise: a mistrust of the Western way of life, from foreign policy to fast food. What Americans may deem national security, others may label as isolationist fortress America. If you are traveling from the US, you may encounter situations in which you are wise to be low-key and restrained.

Although these trends are on the rise, it is unwise to make any assumptions. It is more prudent to read the Country Profiles in advance and then observe what is happening when you are on the scene. I also suggest checking both the UK and US official sources of travel advice: http://www.fco.gov.uk/ and http://travel.state.gov/. What cannot be over-emphasized is the positive effect you will have if you have done your homework and it is evident you are eager to respect the customs of the country.

The information in the Country Profiles has been collected from clients, graduate business students and friends who have lived, worked and spoken in countries around the world, and is also based upon my experience both as speaker and communications consultant. But, of course, I take full responsibility for errors or omissions.

Before you check out the country where you will be speaking, take a look at the following remarks which put the Country Profile information into perspective.

Time

Originally, respondents were offered a choice of saying "Time is sacred, respected or flexible." As you will see, additional comments are included as appropriate. No matter what the prevailing attitude to time, the best business behavior is to be punctual and also not to get upset if you are subjected to delays. Why not take this copy of *Speaking Globally* to read in case you have to wait?

Names and Titles

In each Country Profile, you will learn the correct form of address to use upon meeting. In most countries, once you have established a relationship, the rules relax, but moving into informality is easier than trying to become more formal. In most countries, avoid the typical American gaffe of saying, "Just call me Jim." If someone gets your name and/or title wrong, correct them gently, as in "My name is Beth Urech, not Beth Zurich. 'Zurich' is where I have one of my offices." *Especially for women:* in some cultures, the designation "Ms." is not well known. Instead of making an issue of it, my advice is to use "Mrs."

Business Cards

Especially if you are traveling to Asia, you will need a large supply of business cards, probably 200 for one week. When you translate them, get a "back translation" from a competent source. That is how I learned that the first attempt at a translation into Mandarin of my Swiss firm's name "Speak for Yourself" was a brusque "Speak up or shut up." I have been assured that the second version is both accurate and elegant. You need a special case just for these cards. Do not just put them in a pocket or billfold.

In Asian cultures, writing on people's business cards in front of them is impolite. To keep track of whom you meet, you need a system. What works for me is the following: I keep my cards in my left jacket pocket and those I receive in my right jacket pocket. As soon as possible, I do write on the cards: where we met, distinguishing features and topics of discussion. If I collect seven business cards at my luncheon table, I note "L" for "Lunch" and numbers one to seven which designate where each person sat.

If you want to get the optimal advantage of an international conference, you have to remember who's who! Then you can call at a later date and say, "We sat across from each other at lunch in Beijing. Your ideas for improving the transportation infrastructure were highly interesting. Could we meet briefly when I am in Hong Kong next week?"

Dress Code

If you are speaking at an international business conference, a conservative suit and tie for men and suit for women are the standard uniform, but subtle touches can make a positive difference.

Toasts

If a meal is part of the festivities of your business trip, you may have the opportunity or the duty to offer a toast. How nice if you can do it appropriately and with charm. If you receive a toast, you will be more at ease if you know how to respond. In any case, being able to say "cheers" in the language of the country is always appreciated. Do refer to Chapter 11 for general guidelines.

Non-Verbal Communication

Studies show that our bodies speak louder than we do. That is why having a general idea of what is accepted in a country is only the beginning. Obviously, in many countries, a back-slapping sort of fellow will need to tone down his exuberance. On the other hand, if you are reserved and diffident, you may need to upgrade or you will be left out. Whether eye contact is generally direct or indirect, when you are speaking you need to look at your audience. The significance of gestures varies from one place to another. The classic example is the "A-OK" gesture which is positive in the USA and obscene in much of the rest of the world. Two gestures which seem to be universally despised are pointing a finger at someone or standing with your arms across your chest in an arrogant stance.

Your Speech

Begin By Speaking in the Language of the Country

In asking people how best to build a connection, the overwhelming answer was to begin with a few words in the language of the country. Of course, you need to ask someone on the scene to help you with the pronunciation.

Showing your local hosts the Country Profile helps them understand what you are trying to do and may spark some enlightening comments.

> When Yuri Lustenberger-Kim read, "It is a pleasure to be here," she commented that in Korea it is better to thank your audience for honoring you with their presence. Koreans are taught to focus on the act which is worthy of attention. Instead of telling them that you are delighted to be in Korea, thank them for their attendance which thereby allows you to speak.

Greeting VIPs When You Begin Speaking

The local custom as well as the formality of the event will determine whether or not to greet every VIP by name. The best policy is to be fully prepared. If you notice no one else is doing it, my advice would be to jettison this custom because it does slow down your message!

Humor

To paraphrase poet Robert Frost, "Humor is usually what gets lost in translation." In fact, as you will read, in some countries you are well advised not to attempt humor in any shape or form.

Sensitive Issues

You cannot be expected to know all the ins and outs of local politics and political correctness, but at least try to put your best foot forward, not in your mouth.

Audience Response and Participation

> During my first conference in Hungary, I was puzzled to see men leaving in pairs and returning about five minutes later. When I checked it out, I learned they were just having a smoker's break and a little chat at the same time. That was reassuring. I had been afraid they were upset.
>
> At the Davos World Economic Forum, the tendency of Asians to close their eyes in the audience was openly discussed because non-Asians found it disconcerting until they were assured it is acceptable behavior for people who are used to listening to tonal languages.

Especially for Women

From my perspective, women adapt amazingly well in new environments because they are sensitive and because they "look before they leap." These comments are included to make your leap a bit easier.

Comments

Certainly not inclusive, these comments touch upon a multitude of issues and will give you an edge in a new country.

If your country is not listed or you have additions or changes, please contact me so we can include them in the next edition!

Argentina

1. In the business world, you should arrive on *time*, however you may have to wait. For social occasions, check to find out if the event is expected to start on time. Some Argentineans work late hours. Do not be surprised if a meeting is scheduled for 7 p.m. or later.

2. First *names* are usually used upon meeting, but it is important to follow your host's lead. In spoken communication, *titles* may be used with surnames, such as Doctor (for a Ph.D. or physician), *Ingeniero* (for an engineer), Professor (for a teacher) and *Abogado* (for an attorney). If a CEO does not have such a title, he (or she) will appreciate being addressed as *"Señor"* (or *"Señora"*).

3. *Business cards* are exchanged upon meeting. Argentineans will have cards in Spanish and English.

4. In the business world, you *greet* by shaking hands.

5. *Business dress code* for men is a dark suit and tie although they wear lighter colors in summer. Light colors may be worn during the day and dark colors at night. Argentinean women wear suits, pants, short dresses, mini skirts, light and colorful.

6. To make a *toast*, say *"quisiera prononer un Brindis."* Then say a few words about the hospitality and the success of the business, *"Por su hospitalidad y el éxito de nuestro negocio."* If you receive a toast, say *"Salud"* and repeat the above sentence or say *"muchas gracias."*

7. *Non-verbal communication.* People who have an informal manner are appreciated. Eye contact is direct.

8. *Your speech.* To begin in Spanish say, *"Buenos dias/buenas tardes, señoras y señores."* ("Good morning/afternoon, ladies and gentlemen.") Between colleagues, just say *"Buenos dias/buenas tardes."*

   "Es para mi un placer estar aqui, en ..." (name of place) or *"Estoy encantado de estar aqui, en ..."* (it is a pleasure to be here in ...).

Greeting VIPs at the beginning of your speech is customary.

Humor is appreciated if it is witty.

Sensitive issues include the local recession, economic issues, privatization and the Falkland War. Never talk to an Argentinean about local politics.

During your speech, do not be surprised if the audience talks to each other. However, the audience will be well educated and the attention depends upon the speaker.

In your Question & Answer session, expect active participation.

9. *Especially for women*. Women greet women and men by kissing on the cheek if they know each other well. Accept courtesy from men and do not flaunt your feminist flag. (Also true for Chile.)

10. *Comments*. Argentineans will be pleased if you refer to the beauty of the country and your knowledge about their white wine and sports figures in soccer, tennis and horseracing.

Australia

1. *Time* is respected.

2. First *names* are used on meeting with people of equal rank, except when speaking to a senior person in government or the elderly. *Titles* are not used in spoken communication.

3. *Business cards* may be exchanged upon meeting.

4. In the business world, you *greet* by shaking hands.

5. *Business dress code* for men is dark suit and tie.

   Business dress code for women is suit, or jacket. Trousers are very acceptable; dresses are popular. Stockings need not be worn in hot climates but are worn otherwise. Colors for women are flexible. Black is popular in Melbourne, but fashionably bright or pastel colors are popular all over Australia.

6. Making a *toast* is quite informal.

   If you receive a toast, say 'thank you.'

7. *Non-verbal communication.* Australians like people who are open and easy-going. Eye contact is direct. Avoid grand hand gestures or pointing. Don't stand too close.

8. *Your speech.* Greeting VIPs at the beginning is customary.

   Humor is appreciated it if is witty but avoid jokes about women, Irish, aborigines, racism, minorities.

   Sensitive issues include aboriginal land rights, religion, racism, Australia becoming a republic, boat people, Iraq.

   During your speech, do not be surprised if your audience spontaneously asks questions.

   In your Question & Answer session, your audience may or may not participate so be prepared for either. The questions may be quite informal.

9. *Especially for women.* Women are quite frequent as speakers and are well-accepted in the business world. Extending your arm to shake hands can increase your sense of presence.

10. *Comments.* Since Australian news is often not covered internationally, reading an Australian newspaper in flight or upon arrival will help you learn about current events. Australia's multi-cultural society is seen in people's names, appearances, dress, food and language and is considered to be a great asset in capital cities, but a more reserved view is often found in country towns. Be 'politically correct' and gender inclusive in your speech (i.e., use feminine pronouns and references.) Women prefer to be called "women," but "ladies" is acceptable. "Girls" is too familiar in a business context but may be used socially between women. Foreign business and professional visitors are warmly received and respected, but there are few interpreters, so fluent English is expected, unless at a specifically multicultural function.

    Australian culture has strong British roots but modern Australians adopt much of the culture of the USA. However, they are sensitive to the US domination of the media, so if you are an American speaker, be respectful and sensitive to cultural differences. You do not want to be seen as glib, superficial or loud.

Austria

1. *Time* is rather flexible, less strict than in Germany or Switzerland. Meetings will start punctually and you should not come late or early!

2. In a city, use surnames and titles. *Titles* are very important to Austrians and they will be pleased if you use them with surname. Boss/employee relationships may not progress to first names. Listen and follow the lead of others around you. In the Tyrol, you may move to first names quickly.

3. *Business cards* are exchanged when you meet.

4. In the business world, you shake hands both when *greeting* and leaving. Women should offer their hand first. Handshakes should be firm and with direct eye contact. It is considered rude to have your hands in your pockets while you are being introduced or while talking to anyone.

5. *Business dress code* for men is a suit. Always a tie. Never remove your jacket without asking permission of any women who are present. Do not dress better than your superior. *Business dress code* for women is either a tailored suit or dress with jacket. Light colors may be worn during the day and dark colors at night. Stockings are worn. Avoid flashy colors. If going to the theatre or opera, the wearing of dinner jackets for men and evening dresses for women is not uncommon.

6. The host makes the *toast*. If that is you, say a few words and end with *"Prost"* or *"Prosit."* Look at each person in the eye around the table, giving a slight nod and then drinking. Clinking glasses is usually only done at special occasions.

7. *Non-verbal communication*. Austrians like people who are well-dressed and polite. Anecdotally, Austrians greet everyone when entering and leaving shops and doctors' offices (not just the store clerk or receptionist.) Their manners are traditional. Austrians frown on excessive touching and proximity. They consider chewing gum to be rude.

8. *Your speech.* Perhaps you would like to begin with *"Gruss Gott"* which is the most common greeting in Austria, as opposed to *"Guten Tag"* which is heard in Germany.

   Greet VIPs at the beginning of your speech with their titles, for example, *"Herr Bundeskanzler"* and *"Frau Direktor."*

   If you want to include humor, you may use a self-deprecating comment. If you are from Germany or Switzerland, jokingly refer to yourself as a *"Piefke"* or *"Preusse"* which are diminutive expressions.

   Sensitive issues include racism, the Third Reich, foreigners, homosexuality, sex, US foreign policy. Avoid any mention of personal finances, boasting or obvious name-dropping. Do not mention Jörg Haider or Kurt Waldheim.

   During your speech, expect polite nodding and smiling.

   In your Q&A session, expect limited participation.

9. *Especially for Women.* Women are well accepted in Austria.

10. *Comments.* Austria is the most romantic German-speaking country in Europe, and the Austrians pride themselves on their warmth and friendliness. Says Linda Spillmann, "Austrians are concerned about the environment, highly educated, not afraid to express their opinions and appreciative of arts and culture. To charm the charming Austrians, attempt to speak a bit of German, be sensitive to their opinions and mention Austrians of historical significance."

Belgium

1. *Time* generally is respected.

2. First *names* cannot usually be used upon meeting, and it usually takes longer to get to first name basis with French speakers than with Flemish speakers. *Titles* are not used in spoken communication, except for the Flemish who use titles such as Doctor.

3. There is no set time to exchange *business cards*.

4. In the business world, you *greet* by shaking hands.

5. *Business dress code* for men is a suit or jacket and tie. *Business dress code* for women is a suit. The French influence in fashion is evident.

6. To make a *toast*, say *"Op Uw gezondheid"* or *"A votre santé,"* depending on whether you are in Flemish or French-speaking company. If you do not know the ethnic origin of your host, using English is safer.

   To respond to a toast, say the same words or "cheers!"

7. *Non-verbal communication.* People who have a formal manner are well received. Eye contact is direct.

   Avoid touching other people.

8. *Your speech.* Opening in Flemish: *"Goedemorgen/Goedenavond, dames en heren."* ("Good morning/evening, ladies and gentlemen.")

   "Het is een genoegen in ... te zijn." ("It is a pleasure to be here . . .")

   Opening in French: *"Bonjour/bonsoir, mesdames et messieurs."* ("Good day, good evening, ladies and gentlemen.")

   "Je suis enchanté/e d'être ici." ("I am delighted to be here.") However, using the incorrect language is worse than using English.

   Greeting VIPs at the beginning of your speech is customary. Here you would use titles like "Chairman" or "President."

   Humor is appreciated if it is witty but avoid jokes about women and the Royal Family or the differences between the Flemish and the Walloons (the French-speaking people).

   Sensitive issues are sex, religion, abortion, corruption and child abuse.

   During your speech, do not be surprised if your audience occasionally talks to each other.

   In your Question & Answer session, expect limited participation. People are reserved, and you may almost have to provoke them if you want a reaction.

9. *Especially for women.* If you behave in a friendly yet reserved manner, you will be well accepted.

10. *Comments.* Two main languages spoken in Belgium: French and Flemish. Brussels is bilingual. German is spoken in the six cities in the southeast of Belgium. If you want to impress your audience, speak

with "esprit," which is witty and dazzles the listener. Some Belgians are quite earthy and might be unimpressed by your flair. However, all Belgians enjoy good food and wine.

Brazil

1. In Sao Paulo you are expected to be on *time* for business meetings. Elsewhere being late is acceptable. For social situations it is normal to be 15-30 minutes late.

2. First *names* are generally not used initially. You may be invited to use someone's first name after the first meeting. The order of names is given name, then surname (father's name) and academic titles are used. In Brazil, when you greet someone you may address them as Senhor or Senhora, but without the surname.

3. *Business cards* are exchanged upon meeting. Translating your card into Portuguese is appreciated.

4. In the business world, men *greet* by shaking hands. It is important to shake hands with everyone in a group. Women often greet each other by kissing on each cheek with what is known as an "air kiss."

5. *Business dress code* for men is a dark suit and classic tie in Sao Paulo, Brasilia and Porto Allegre. It is more casual in Rio. *Business dress code* for women is a suit. Trouser suits are very popular. Avoid flashy colors.

6. To make a *toast*, say, "*Saúde.*" Reply with "*Saúde.*" Among friends, you can say, "*Tim tim.*"

7. *Non-verbal communication.* Upon meeting, you should have a formal manner. Eye contact is direct. Avoid the "A-OK" gesture which is considered obscene.

8. *Your speech.* Opening: "*Bom dia/boa tarde, senhoras e senhores.*" It is a great pleasure to be here: "*é um grande prazer estar aqui em Sao Paulo/ no Rio de Janeiro,*" "*estou encantada (feminine) encantado (masculine) de estar aqui em Sao Paulo/ no Rio Janeiro.*"

Greeting VIPs at the beginning of your speech is an absolute necessity, especially your host or hosts.

Sensitive issues include politics and minorities. Glowing comments about Brazilian women are not appreciated.

Humor is fine if you avoid jokes about religion. A joke about yourself is a good ice-breaker as long as it isn't forced.

During your speech, do not be surprised if your audience asks questions or talks to each other.

In your Question & Answer session, expect lively participation.

9. *Especially for women.* You will enjoy Brazilian hospitality. You are cautioned to avoid having dinner with just one man as it may be misinterpreted.

10. *Comments.* Portuguese is the language in Brazil (not Spanish). It is remarkably different from the Portuguese spoken in Portugal, especially in pronunciation. What you can do to really impress your audience is say a few words in Brazilian Portuguese or cite a Brazilian writer. Take note that in Sao Paulo, people are very well educated. After the first meeting except in Sao Paulo, greetings and good-byes are warm with effusive handshaking or a hand on your shoulder. Brazilians are friendly people—take their lead in any meeting or social situation. By and large they are receptive to Americans and love to talk about US cities. Music is their passion, as are soccer and car racing.

Bulgaria

1. *Time* is money (*"vremeto e pari"*).

2. First *names* such as Vasil, Dimitar, Boitsho (male) or Rada, Borjana, Dessislava (female) are used as soon as familiarity has been established. Last names such as Petkov, Dragostinov, Ivanov end with an additional — a if used by women: Petkova, etc. *Titles* are used when addressing a person in a formal way, e.g. in front of an audience.

3. *Business cards* are exchanged upon shaking hands.

4. *Greeting* is by handshake, usually initiated by the person entering the room.

5. Suit and tie for men, suit or pant suit for women are the appropriate *attire* for *business* meetings.

6. The *toast 'nasdrave'* is answered with the same word.

7. Bulgarians are open people who like direct eye contact and appreciate politeness and punctuality as a *non-verbal* show of respect.

8. *Your speech*. Begin your speech with *'dobar den'* (good day) followed by *'dobre deshli'* (welcome) and, if appropriate, preceded by *'uvashaemidami I gospoda'* (Ladies and gentlemen).

   When greeting VIPs, which is customary, hierarchy has to be painstakingly respected.

   Humor is appreciated but must be used with caution.

   A Bulgarian audience is rather generous with applause while remaining critical and making exacting use of the Question & Answer session.

9. *Especially for women*. Bulgarian women have long ago attained equal rights in terms of salaries and access to executive positions. Many women have a university education and most of them work. Today's career women rely upon and are grateful for the help of stay-at-home grandmothers. If they treat men with respect laced with a touch of arrogance, it is because they marshal career, social events and family life so supremely.

10. *Comments*. Bulgarians dislike being cornered and react with expressions like *'shte vidim!'* (we'll see about that).

    In the Eastern bloc, Soviets imposed division of labor and Bulgarians were arbitrarily allocated the engineering function. As a result engineering schools frequented by students of varying capabilities sprang up throughout the country, even in the most remote areas. The result was the creation of the comical character *'Engineer Ganev,'* an incompetent, piteous and perpetually exhausted fellow who is the brunt of many jokes.

Cameroon

1. *Time* is flexible. If your speech is scheduled to begin at 3 p.m., do not be surprised if people wander in half an hour late.

2. In a business context, people are very formal. Always use surnames with *titles*, including Mr., Mrs., Doctor and Professor.

3. *Business cards* are exchanged after the meeting or during a social time. Be sure to include your educational qualifications (BA, MA) as well as your job title.

4. Cameroon was settled by the French and the English. The differences are noticeable in how one *greets*. In English-speaking areas, shaking hands is the rule. In the French areas, there is more kissing on cheeks.

5. *Business dress code* for men is either traditional outfit or a suit. Business dress code for women is a suit. Trousers are not acceptable. Don't be fancy, be sedate. Avoid black which is a sign of mourning. Also avoid the combination red and black which signifies disaster. A black suit with white blouse is fine. When you are the speaker, choose something more colorful. Bare legs are fine.

6. To make a *toast*, say, "I would like to make a toast" and add a few words. Women do not generally make toasts.

   If you receive a toast, respond graciously and acknowledge your guest givers.

7. *Non-verbal communication*. People embrace readily. Just observe and see what others do. Eye contact is important.

8. *Your speech*. Greeting: Since there are two hundred languages in Cameroon and not a national language, use English. If you are speaking in a French area, start with a word or two in French and then apologize if you must continue in English.

   You will sense the French influence in protocol. Recognizing dignitaries is necessary. Mention the most important members in your audience by title and name in descending order, beginning with the governors of the province. After greeting the first five personally, you can refer to the other VIPs as "distinguished."

Humor: If your audience looks receptive, you can lighten up, but not a lot.

Sensitive issues: Politics, religion, personal matters. Cameroon has a high incidence of HIV, up to two-thirds of males aged 15-29 are infected. Tread lightly.

Audience reaction and participation: Be keenly observant. Expect moderate reactions and applause.

In a Question & Answer session, you can throw it open to questions. If you are naturally exuberant, be sedate in order to win respect.

9. *Especially for women.* Be reserved, but not rigid. You will be respected if you abide by local customs. Never cross your legs. Some people take great exception to this. When you are sitting at a table or desk, don't rest your head on your hand. This signals that you are upset or worried, and you risk someone knocking your hand away.

10. *Comments.* Cameroon is the size of California and has almost 20 million people in 200 ethnic groups. Maryann M. Mukete, Director of Women's Empowerment in Kumba, says, "Cameroon is like Africa in miniature. We have deserts, rain forests, grasslands, coastlands. The variety of peoples who inhabit these areas is diverse."

Canada

1. *Time* is respected.

2. First *names* can be used with people of equal rank but play it safe and wait for the invitation. With the elderly or the powerful, use "Mr.", "Ms." or "Mrs.", followed by last name, in English-speaking Canada. Use *"Monsieur"* and *"Madame"* with last name in French-speaking Canada. In spoken communication, *titles* are not normally used except for doctors, ministers and judges.

3. *Business cards* are exchanged upon meeting.

4. In the business world, you *greet* by shaking hands.

5. Until recently *business dress code* for men was a dark suit and tie. In the Western provinces, it was a jacket and open-collared shirt. Now it's best to check ahead. Women can also

check ahead, however they will be fine in a suit, trouser suit or dress. Skirt not too short and stockings, please.

6. To make a *toast*, raise your glass and say, "I would like to toast . . ." If you receive a toast, give a small thank you speech.

7. *Non-verbal communication.* Canadians like people who have an open and friendly manner. Eye contact is direct. Avoid pointing or using any grand gestures.

8. *Your speech.* If you are speaking in French-speaking Canada, a few introductory words in French would be appreciated.

   Greeting VIPs at the beginning of your speech is customary.

   Currently a large percentage of top English-speaking comedians are Canadian, a good indication that humor is enjoyed, particularly if it is clever and dry. However, it is best to avoid jokes about sex, politics, religion and minorities.

   During your speech, your audience will pay attention.

   In your Question & Answer session, expect limited participation until the audience gets warmed up. Then participation can get lively.

9. *Especially for women.* Women will be treated the same as men. In some sessions, particularly confrontational ones, they are appreciated for their manner and outlook.

10. *Comments.* Although they share a 3,000-mile long border, Canadians do not appreciate being called Americans or confused with them. Canadians are nice and polite, often rather conservative, and operate on the basis of consensus not confrontation. They would be pleased if you mention the beauty of their land and their clean, safe cities. They are proud of their ethnic diversity which they refer to as "a cultural mosaic" not a melting pot (as do their neighbors to the south).

Chile

1. Business people in Chile are generally on *time*, but you may have to wait 10-15 minutes. "We are more punctual than

Argentineans," offers a Chilean respondent, "however in both countries lower echelons will make you wait to feel important."

2. First *names* are often used upon meeting, but you refer to the other person as *"Usted."* Unless you understand when to use *"Don"* and *"Doña,"* don't try. Pay attention to what others are doing.

3. *Business cards* are exchanged before or after meetings.

4. In the business world, men and women *greet* by shaking hands.

5. *Business dress code* for men is a classic and elegant suit. Dark colors are preferred. *Business dress code* for women: trouser suit or regular suit with skirts not much above the knees. No tight or revealing clothes. Avoid white suits, flashy colors or "wacky" ties. Suspenders are not fashionable.

6. To make a *toast*, raise your glass and say a few warm words. If you receive a toast, you are expected to say a few words in return. Do not clink your glass.

7. *Non-verbal communication.* Eye contact is direct. As in other Latin American countries, physical proximity is closer than in North America so you need not feel threatened if someone is "in your space."

8. *Your speech.* To begin in Spanish, say, *"Buenos dias/tardes, Señoras y Señores"* (Good morning/afternoon, ladies and gentlemen). *"Es un verdadero placer de estar con Ustedes"* (It is a pleasure to be here).

Greeting VIPs at the beginning of your speech is customary.

Humor is appreciated if it is relevant to the situation. "Bottled jokes" are considered stupid.

Sensitive issues include politics, territorial rights with Argentina, divorce law in congress. Avoid critical remarks about Chile. Unless you are knowledgeable about the local scene, it is better not to give your opinion.

In your Question & Answer session, expect little participation. It requires considerable effort to get the first question asked. After that, things flow more smoothly.

9. *Especially for women.* Accept courtesy from men and do not flaunt your feminist flag. Men expect to open the door for women and to

pick up a restaurant bill (unless it is a business event and the invitation was extended by the woman).

10. *Comments.* What you can do to impress is to be knowledgeable about Chile, particularly its history and the high quality of its red wine (and the fact that phyloxera did not affect Chilean vineyards). Also you can speak about Chile's improved position vis à vis other Latin American countries.

China

1. *Time* is respected. Be on time but do not arrive terribly early.

2. First *names* are not generally used upon meeting. Traditionally, the surname is first, followed by the first name. Nowadays, you can also say "Mr." or "Mrs." with the surname. *Titles* such as Doctor, Professor, Director and Chairman are used with surname (Deputy Director-General Li). Never drop a title in favor of "Mr." or "Mrs." or "Ms.".

3. *Business cards* should be in your language on one side and Chinese on the other side. When your cards are translated into Chinese, include your title. Your hotel concierge can arrange to have cards printed in both languages within 24 hours (it is not expensive by Western standards). Business cards are exchanged upon meeting. Facing the other person, hold your card in both hands by the two corners on your side with the Chinese side up. When you receive your counterpart's card, look at it respectfully but do not write on it. At a meeting you may arrange cards on the table in front of you. Afterwards, put them in your cardholder carefully. Do not write with red ink in China.

4. In the business world, you *greet* by shaking right hands. Handshakes tend not to be very firm but often are accompanied by a slight bow.

5. *Business dress code* for men is suit or jacket and tie. *Business dress code* for women is suit, trouser suit or dress. Dark or neutral colors are best. Avoid white or bright colors which are considered aggressive.

Chinese people on the mainland generally dress more casually than Westerners both in business, concerts and social events. In Hong Kong, men and women are fashion conscious and dress very well.

6. If you receive a *toast*, it is polite to say a few words of appreciation. If you are hosting an event, toast guests according to rank or title, beginning with the highest level. Chinese may clink glasses. The Chinese toast is *"Gan bei"* which literally means "drain your glass." If someone says *"Gan bei,"* you should drink as much as he does and say *"Xie Xie,"* "thank-you," pronounced shay-shay. One way to get around this situation is to say *"Sui Yi."* It means you can drink as much as you like, but make sure the other party understands your intentions.

7. *Non-verbal communication.* As Jon Anderson, Partner in Chicago-based ChinaLine LLC points out, "Social distance is much closer in China than in most Western countries, so expect that the Chinese may intrude often into your personal space. The Chinese place a great emphasis on 'harmony' so even though you may see some Chinese get quite excited in non-formal situations, they will almost always be quite hospitable and non-confrontational in business settings." Chinese like people who are respectful. Once the Chinese get to know you, they can be "touchy-feely," but it is best if you are very polite until you know them. Eye contact is direct. Lack of eye-contact does not convey insincerity but is a way of showing respect. Never put your feet on the table, do not raise your "pinkie finger." Avoid any aggressive gesture. Don't laugh loudly. Chinese women will often cover their mouths and avert their eyes when laughing.

8. *Your speech.* Begin with "Welcome, guests/friends," *"Huan ying ge wei"*: (guests) *ke ren*/(friends) *peng you*.

   Make a point of greeting Chinese VIPs beginning with the highest in rank.

   Humor is appreciated but be careful in telling jokes which may not get interpreted appropriately. Avoid jokes about their language, customs or sex.

   Sensitive issues include human rights, sex, politics, crime, religion, Chinese relationships with the USA, Tibet and Hong Kong/Taiwan issues.

In your Question & Answer session, you can stimulate participation by asking your own staff to initiate one or two questions. Many Chinese people are shy at opening up discussions but can be quite open when someone else has spoken up.

9. *Especially for women.* Communism has done a great deal to encourage equality of the sexes, and it is not unusual for a woman to be a leader or owner of a private enterprise. As a Western woman, having dinner or a drink on your own is fine in cities. However, in provincial areas, it is prudent to be conservative. Smoking in public is frowned upon — don't do it in a business setting.

10. *Comments.* Remember that in China, people know you are a foreigner and almost expect you to do things wrong or in a different or amusing way. Play it by ear, observe what goes on around you and have fun! Be patient, as haste arouses suspicion.

Learn some key words in Chinese. Shi Han, Managing Partner of ChinaLine mentions you will gain respect for your attempts to communicate in Chinese, regardless of your level of fluency.

It is important to understand the general principle of "saving face." Causing a business partner to lose face will have devastating effects. The Chinese may not say "no" to you to avoid your losing face. Many negotiations have been endlessly delayed because of this, so try to get the real answer by subtle means. Conversely "giving face" through compliments is valued but do not single out an individual in a group since this may backfire and embarrass a higher up who is present. Note these comments apply to ethnic Chinese in Singapore and Malaysia, too.

Croatia

1. Although you should always be punctual, Croatians may be late. You should expect to wait about 15 minutes.

2. Croatians love formality. It is proper business etiquette to address Croatians using their last *names*. Croatians are very sensitive to the use of *titles*, such as professor, doctor and other professional degrees. For individuals who have Master's Degrees, use the title

"Magistar," with stress on the middle syllable. If an individual has more than one degree, use the more important one.

3. *Business cards* are used by everyone in Croatia—from cab driver to Managing Director. Even high school students carry cards, and they are handed out readily. When attending a formal meeting, it is appropriate to exchange cards at the beginning and then place the cards you receive in front of you on the table.

4. Business people shake hands when meeting.

5. Foreign business visitors to Croatia are advised to *dress* formally. However, there are two different standards for Croatian business attire.

In an international business setting, older and serious businesspeople will be formally attired. Men wear suits or jackets and ties, and business women wear suits or dresses and high heels. Particularly in the capital city of Zagreb, business people dress very fashionably. They purchase expensive accessories, like briefcases, scarves, watches and jewelry. Seeing and being seen is important!

However, younger "anti-establishment" generation may appear casual, wearing jeans with unusual ties and accessories.

6. At the end of a meeting, *toasts* are obligatory if a deal is completed. Typically, the toast is given by the Croatian host and champagne is served. A business lunch or dinner also starts with a toast, and it is appropriate for you as the foreign visitor to make the toast. When you clink your glass, it is crucial to look directly in the eyes of the other person. Not doing so is a sign of rudeness and insincerity. Americans often avert eyes and clink glasses quickly which is considered a major *faux pas*. To toast, say *zivjeli* (to life) or *nazdravlje* (to your health).

7. Croatians are very impressed by titles, education, company names, and connections. The Croatian host is sensitive as to who sits next to foreigner business guests as it is a pleasure to sit close to them.

8. Croatians will not expect you to speak Croatian but will be happy and respectful if you manage a few words like beginning your speech with *"dobro jutro"* (good morning), *"dobar dan"* (good afternoon) and *"kako ste?"* (how are you?).

Croatians do have a good sense of humor, and light-hearted comments which encourage a relaxing environment are welcome.

Sensitive issues. Steer clear of Croatian politics. Croatians are extremely opinionated on the historical and political aspects of the recent war with Serbia leading to Croatia's independence. It is best not to voice any opinion on it. Please note that their language is Croatian, not Serbo-Croatian.

During your speech, Croatians, who are very curious, will pay attention and ask questions.

9. Kathleen Gaber, attorney with Masuda, Funai, Eifert and Mitchell, Ltd. says, "Croatian businesswomen are a pleasure to work with— open, honest, genuine, well-educated and largely equal in the business arena. In fact, the government is 24% women. As a foreign business woman, you should expect men to open doors, pull out your chair and occasionally stare or even flirt with you. Maintaining a professional and somewhat aloof manner will dissuade their attention."

10. *Comments*. If agreements are made, get them in writing. Be sure this person has the authority to authorize the agreement as many Croatians tend to exaggerate in order to impress, and they may offer something that they cannot provide.

Because Croatia has only been independent since 1991, the democratic mentality of people is still evolving. Many lower-level bureaucrats still expect a favor or remuneration, particularly for moving paperwork through the system—a throw-back to the former Communist regime.

Croatians are warm and hospitable. It would not be uncommon for them to invite you to their home or show you around their city. Do not be surprised if after a few drinks, they give you a warm pat on the back. It's their Mediterranean temperament.

As Lovorka Ostrunic, Acting Consul General, says, "We are proud because we are an old nation with a rich past. We like to talk about our culture, ethnicity and history."

Czech Republic

1. Being punctual is appreciated, but Czechs are often late and certainly more relaxed about *time* than their German neighbors.

2. First *names* are usually not used at the first meeting. In the Czech Republic, women's last names end with *"ova."* So a foreign woman attending a conference should not be surprised to see her name written with *"ova,"* as in Elizabeth Urechova. *Titles* are a must. When speaking about someone, refer to the person using their title and surname. When addressing the person face-to-face, use the title without surname.

3. *Business cards* are important — and are given with pride (because for 40 years they did not have any). Business cards list as many titles and academic credentials as you can muster. Exchanging cards at the beginning of a meeting ensures that all parties see how each other's names are written and makes for easier retention. Don't hesitate to take the initiative in offering your card.

4. You *greet* by shaking hands and saying *"Dobry den"* (Good day). When greeting, use titles, too. *"Dobry den, pane inzenyre"* (Good day, Mr. Engineer.)

5. *Business dress code* is the same as in Western Europe although trends are not followed as closely and some outfits may appear slightly out of date. Personal grooming may not always meet your standards; be understanding. Sometimes, styles might be a little overdone, but a certain Slavic "chic" is to be expected.

6. *Toasts* are often made. At a bare minimum, raise your glass and say *"Na zdravi!"* Clink glasses with the people nearest to you while looking into their eyes. If the table is very large, you can raise your glass slightly and nod your head at the people farther away.

7. *Non-verbal communication.* The Czechs talk with their eyes and hands. That's normal.

8. *Your speech.* To begin your speech in Czech, say *"Vážené dámy a pánové"* or *"Vážení přátelé"* Of course, check with a Czech for correct pronunciation.

The audience at a chemical conference warmed to Max Robinson when he began: *"As a boy, I played the clarinet in my school orchestra. My favorite music was the New World Symphony. I never dreamt that one day I would be speaking in the country where Dvorak was born."* Max also mentioned Czech Nobel Prize winners and his love for Czech beer. With these three references, he made a powerful connection! In social conversation or to warm up the audience — you also can mention some good names in tennis or hockey.

Greeting VIPS is very important.

Humor will be appreciated. The Czechs have their own variety of so-called black humor which ranges from charming to rough.

Sensitive issues include former Russian occupation, the relationship with Slovakia and minorities.

Audience participation. Some still hesitate to speak in an open forum. For forty years they were told what to think and do. As a speaker, if you want audience involvement, you can begin by having your moderator ask you questions which you have prepared in advance. After you answer each question, you (or the moderator) can ask for comments or more questions. Thus encouraged, your listeners will begin raising their hands, and you will have a lively interchange.

9. *Especially for women.* Czech women still tolerate suggestive comments and behavior from their male counterparts. However, Czech men are aware that this is inappropriate towards a woman from another country. Behave with decorum, and you should have no problems.

10. *Comments.* Mention contributions the Czechs have made to the world: elegant classical music, Prague, great hockey and tennis players. They are very proud of Karl's University, the first German-speaking university in Central Europe, which was founded in 1348.

Denmark

1. *Time* is respected.

2. First *names* can be used upon meeting. *Titles* are not normally used in spoken communication.

3. There is no set standard for exchanging *business cards.*

4. In the business world, you *greet* by shaking hands.

5. *Business dress code* for men is dark suit or jacket and tie. *Business dress code* for women is suit or trouser suit with long sleeves. Avoid flashy bright colors.

6. To make a *toast,* say a few words ending with "*skål.*" If you receive a toast, maintain eye contact with the person toasting you for a few seconds before nodding in appreciation. You may then say a few words ending with "*skål.*" In both cases, you first look the person in the eye, then drink and look at the person again. You may want to give a subtle tilt with your glass at the end. At a dinner, toasts will occur several times, so avoid emptying your glass completely in between.

7. *Non-verbal communication.* Danes like people who have an informal manner. Eye contact is direct.

8. *Your speech.* Opening in Danish: "*God morgen/god aften, mine damer og herrer*" (good morning/evening, ladies and gentlemen). "*Det er mig en stor fornøjelse at være her i ...*" (It's a pleasure to be here in ...).

   Unless they are very important, greeting VIPs at the beginning of your speech is not customary.

   Humor is appreciated if it is dry, even "black."

   The Danes are open and forthright, and sensitive issues are few outside class differences and possibly the monarchy.

   During your speech, do not be surprised if your audience asks questions or talks to each other quietly.

   In your Question & Answer session, expect limited participation.

9. *Especially for women.* You will be well treated in Denmark but may have to make a stand to gain respect.

10. *Comments.* Danish people appreciate being complimented on their openness and informality. If you are offered coffee and sweets at a meeting, you are expected to at least try them.

Egypt

1. In the business world you are expected to be on *time*, although you may have to wait for higher ranking managers. It is common to set a starting time for a meeting and leave the end open. Socially, usually no specific time is set; people agree to meet "in the evening." If a time is set, you should arrive a bit late. Amany Asfour adds, "In the morning, we are formal. At night our dinners are informal, filled with music and laughter."

2. When meeting people for the first time, use first *names* preceded by Mr., Mrs. or Dr. In spoken communication titles such as Doctor (for a Ph.D. or physician), Bash-Mohandes (Engineer, Architect), and Professor are used. Technicians' names are often preceded by Bash-Mohandes. *Titles* are important. Informally, the long-abolished Turkish titles are still in use, such as Bey and Pasha. Women do not take their husband's name when they marry.

3. *Business cards* are exchanged, usually at the beginning of a meeting. Your card should be in Arabic on one side.

4. In the business world, you *greet* by shaking hands. Religious Muslims do not shake hands with members of the opposite sex. People of the same gender who know each other well may kiss each other on the cheeks. Western women should not initiate shaking hands.

5. *Business dress code* is a suit and tie for men, and a suit or trouser suit for women. When it is hot, women may wear short sleeves. Religious Muslim women are veiled and usually wear long dresses.

6. *Toasts* are not common as the majority of the population is Muslim and does not drink alcohol. In a setting where alcohol is served, Egyptians have no problem toasting with juice or water.

7. *Non-verbal communication* is common and gestures are often used. The specific intention behind some verbal communication such as *"Insha Allah"* (God willing), which may mean yes or no, can only be deciphered using voice intonations and body language. Pointing is rude. People stand at close distances. Do not back off.

8. *Your speech.* You begin by saying *"Saidatee, Anisatee, Sadatee* (Ladies/Mrs., Ladies/Misses, and Gentlemen), *Sabah or Masaa El Kheir* (Good morning or good evening)". Muslims start by saying *"As salamu alaykum"* (Peace be with you). Greeting VIPs and distinguished guests at the beginning of a speech is customary. Humor is very much appreciated. Sensitive issues are religion, sex, politics, Israel. Applause is expected at the end of a speech.

9. *Especially for women.* Amany Asfour explains, "Many misconceptions exist about our culture. Egyptian women receive equal pay and have excellent opportunities in the work force. Our Prophet Mohammed's wife was an independent merchant when they were married. Still, in social gatherings, it is common for men and women to split into separate groups."

10. *Comments.* Omar Mahmoud comments that "Interaction in foreign and joint venture organizations is more liberal than dealing with the state sector." Use of language is flexible. "Tomorrow" does not necessarily imply within 24 hours. It may be a polite way of saying 'never.' Work may be interrupted to perform prayers.

Finland

1. *Time* is extremely respected. Be on time! If you are going to be even five minutes late, you should call in advance.

2. Finns find it awkward if someone uses their first *name* upon meeting. The order of names is given name, surname. *Titles* are not used in spoken communication.

3. *Business cards* are exchanged when you meet, but not in any special manner.

4. In the business world, you *greet* by shaking hands. Don't touch the person with your other hand.

5. For important meetings, *business dress code* for men is a dark suit and tie. A jacket and tie is acceptable except for very high-level meetings. *Business dress code* for women is suit with skirt or trousers. Remember winter!

6. To make a *toast*, say *"Kippis."*

   To respond to a toast, say *"Kippis."* Eye contact should be as your glass is lifted and after you take a drink.

7. *Non-verbal communication*. Eye contact is direct but keep some distance. Avoid broad gestures. Finns tolerate long moments of silence.

8. *Your speech*. Finnish is a difficult language, but you can begin by saying *"Hyvaa Paivaa"* ("Hello") if you practice beforehand.

   Greeting VIPs when you begin speaking is not customary.

   Humor is appreciated if it is understandable.

   Finns can tolerate long periods of silence, so do not worry about filling in the empty spaces.

   During your speech, do not be surprised if your audience is passive.

   In your Question & Answer session, expect little participation.

9. *Especially for women*. Finland was the first European country with women's right to vote. Women are well represented as ministers and in the parliament as well as in business.

10. *Comments*. If you can include some facts about Finnish history and its "sauna-culture," you will impress your audience. The Finns are keen on nature and outdoor activities, so talking about fishing, skiing or ice hockey can be an "ice-breaker." They will appreciate mention of Paavo Nurmi or Lasse Viren (long-distance runners) or their famous footballers Jari Litmanen and Sami Hyypiä. Finland is rich in music. Sibelius is certainly the most famous composer, and Finns would assume you also know their contempory composers Kaija Saariaho and Magnus Lindberg. Six percent of the population has Swedish as a mother-tongue.

France

1. *Time* is more flexible in the southern part of France than in the north.

2. First *names* are not used upon meeting. The French use

"Madame" and *"Monsieur"* without the surname. *Titles* are not normally used in spoken communication, except for *"Docteur"* and *"Professeur."* The French sometimes introduce themselves with their last name first. If you are in doubt, ask. The French say *"Bon jour"* at the beginning of verbal exchanges with hotel clerks, shop assistants, etc. and appreciate your doing so.

3. *Business cards* are exchanged when you meet. Have your card translated into French. Treat your business partners' business cards with respect. Include academic credentials.

4. In the business world, you *greet* by shaking hands.

5. *Business dress code* for men is a dark suit and tie. *Business dress code* for women is a suit. Avoid wearing aggressive colors like yellow and red. It is important to be correctly dressed. Many French resist the American "dress down" style.

6. To make a *toast*, say *"À votre santé."* If you receive a toast, you can toast your host.

7. *Non-verbal communication.* French like people who have a formal manner. Eye contact is quite direct.

8. *Your speech.* To begin in French, say *"Bonjour, mesdames et messieurs."* (Hello, ladies and gentlemen.) *"Je suis enchanté/ée d'être ici."* (I am delighted to be here.)

   Greeting VIPs at the beginning of your speech is not customary.

   Humor is appreciated if it has a light touch.

   Sensitive issues are different ethnic groups, politics, USA, Iraq.

   During your speech, do not be surprised if your audience talks to each other.

   In your Question & Answer session, expect limited participation. The French are rather reserved.

9. *Especially for women.* Women are well accepted in the business world. However, do not mistake gallantry for anything else.

10. *Comments.* What you can do to really impress is to include several correctly enunciated French words and show your knowledge of French wine, history and literature. For the French, *"tout le monde"*

means France and the French language. Most French deplore the fact that English is the lingua franca of the business world so if you can speak in French, you will win their favor. If you make the effort, they will accept your errors. Other than that, they enjoy spirited and lively presentations, but your logic must be sound.

Germany

1. *Time* is sacred. Be punctual!
2. First *names* cannot be used upon meeting, but if you are an American, they may use their first name, in which case, respond in kind. *Titles* are not normally used in spoken communication, except Doctor.
3. *Business cards* are exchanged upon meeting.
4. In the business world, you *greet* by shaking hands.
5. *Business dress code* for men is a dark suit or jacket with tie. *Business dress code* for women is a suit or trouser suit. Short sleeved jackets may be worn in warm weather. Stockings are customary. Avoid flashy colors.
6. To make a *toast* give a small speech and say, *"Prost."* If you receive a toast, say a few words ending with *"Prost."* Although you do not clink glasses, you do raise your glass and look everyone in the eye.
7. *Non-verbal communication.* Germans like people who have a formal manner. Eye contact is direct.
8. *Your speech.* To begin your speech in German: *"Guten Morgen/ Guten Tag, meine Damen und Herren."* (Good morning/good day, ladies and gentlemen.) *"Ich freue mich heute hier vor Ihnen zu sprechen."* (I am pleased to be speaking to you.)

   Greeting VIPs when you begin speaking is customary.

   It would be inappropriate to begin with a joke.

   Sensitive issues include racism, the Third Reich and sex.

   During your speech, do not be surprised if your audience talks to each other.

In your Question & Answer session, expect limited participation. Don't be surprised if your audience asks you blunt or very direct questions.

9. *Especially for women*. Women are treated as equals to men.

10. *Comments*. What you can do to really impress is to translate your slides into German. Presentations should include historical background information, particularly if it is thorough and comprehensive. Facts, in general, are appreciated but proceed in an orderly manner and quote your sources. A summary is very important. In a Question & Answer session, you will probably be asked where your data are coming from and how you reached your conclusion. Be prepared. Although Germans can be forthright, even blunt, you are advised not to take their directness personally. Afterwards over a beer, they will be friendly. Actually, not all Germans are beer-drinkers; in the Rhine area people prefer wine.

Great Britain

1. *Time* is respected.

2. First *names* are not usually used upon meeting. *Titles* such as "Sir" are used with given names. You would address Sir Richard Branson as "Sir Richard." Lords and ladies are addressed with surname, as in "Lord Marshall" (Chairman of BA who used to be "Sir Colin.") A woman earns the title of "Dame" on her own merit, for example, Dame Maggie Smith.

3. *Business cards* are exchanged upon meeting.

4. In the business world, you *greet* by shaking hands.

5. *Business dress code*. You will not be judged by what you wear, but you will gain credibility if you are well-dressed in a British sense. For men this is a dark suit and tie. Do not wear a regimental school tie unless you attended the school. No jewelry apart from a good watch and cufflinks. Well-worn suits are fine as long as they started out well-made. *Business dress code* for women is a tailored suit, coordinates or dress. Colors are more subdued than in the US. Pants suits are popular and acceptable.

6. To make a *toast*, give a short speech. If you receive a toast, you are expected to thank the person who toasted you or to propose a toast to him or her. At official dinners, a toast to the monarchy is given. The host rises and says, "Ladies and gentlemen, the Queen." Then guests rise and respond, "The Queen."

7. *Non-verbal communication.* The British are generally reserved and do not appreciate an aggressive or "hard-sell" approach. Eye contact is direct.

8. *Your speech.* Greeting VIPs at the beginning of your speech is customary.

   Humor is appreciated particularly if it is clever and self-deprecating.

   Sensitive issues include the European Union, mad cow disease, the Iraq War and in some circles, the monarchy.

   During your speech, do not be surprised if your audience does not respond. If your arguments are weak or fatuous, your audience will notice but will be too polite to mention it.

   In Question and Answer sessions, expect moderate participation.

9. *Especially for women.* You will be well-accepted if you are credible. Act with quiet authority and avoid looking too frilly or feminine. Keep hair and make-up simple.

10. *Comments.* Keep in mind the British love of understatement. Their ideal speaker is authoritative and witty. The British are modest and have a dislike of "blowing your own trumpet." Although, they appreciate quality graphics and multi-media presentations, avoid going OTT (over the top).

    While a friendly manner is appreciated, too much informality is frowned upon. If you are American, your accent will be commented upon. Smile and lower the volume. The United Kingdom of Great Britain consists of England, Scotland, Wales and Northern Ireland. Ireland refers to the Republic of Ireland and is a separate country. When referring to the entire region, say Great Britain or United Kingdom which is frequently shortened to "the UK." Refer to the people as "British." Do not refer to a Scottish person as "English."

Greece

1. Punctuality is not a Greek tradition. Arriving 30-45 minutes late for a social meeting is quite acceptable; however, you are expected to arrive on *time* for a business meeting.

2. In business meetings or with older people, use Mr. or Mrs. with surname. You will win points if you address a corporate executive with his *title*. For example, "Mr. President plus surname." You can address people by their first *name* in a social context and if you are the same age.

3. *Business cards* are exchanged at the beginning of a meeting. There is no standardized etiquette on how the exchange is done.

4. Men and women *greet* each other by shaking hands when they first meet or in business settings. However, as you get to know your Greeks, it is acceptable at the end of a social gathering for the men to kiss the women on the cheek. Women also tend to greet each other like this. Do not be surprised if you see men kissing each other but be aware that this is only done between close friends and relatives. Usually you kiss the left cheek first then the right. If you are not careful, you may accidentally kiss on the mouth, something that is not done even between parents and children.

5. *Business dress code* for men is a suit or jacket with tie. In the summer, men can go to a social function with a dress shirt and no jacket. Usually, the appropriate dress code for the evening is agreed beforehand. Do not hesitate to ask. Summer evenings tend to be hot and most restaurants are in the open air. *Business dress code* for women is a suit or trouser suit. In the summer, women tend to wear lighter colors and short sleeves. In business settings, dress conservatively if you want to avoid the stare of men. Greek men assume that foreign women are "easier" to get than Greek women (the legacy of tourism in Greece).

6. To give a *toast*, look at people directly in the eye, raise your glass and say, "*ya mos.*" (to our health.)

7. *Non-verbal communication.* Greeks like to make eye contact and expect you to look at them during a conversation. Sometimes their conversations become very animated, and it appears as if they

are mad at each other. In fact, raising one's voice demonstrates the passion of one's beliefs and convictions.

8. *Your speech.* Most Greeks speak English. However, beginning in Greek can be a plus!

Speaking in Athens, I began by saying, *"Malene Elizabeth agapo tin Elada."* ("My name is Elizabeth and I love Greece.") From the back of the room, the senior sales dealer shouted, "She's all right!" which greatly increased my credibility!

Greeting VIPs when you begin is necessary.

Some humor is OK but focusing on the subject is recommended.

Sensitive Issues. Greek economy is not at par with other industrialized countries of Europe, and Greeks tend to blame everyone else for their predicament. There is a strong anti-American feeling at the present time. The American government is blamed for the Greek civil war, the loss of Cyprus, the unresolved conflict with Turkey and the unjust war in Kosovo. However, Greeks love everything American. They have a problem with the government, not the people of America. Americans will feel welcome and respected in Greece. However, Americans are well advised to stay clear of political discussions.

Expect lively participation during a Q&A session.

9. *Especially for women.* Women have made significant strides in most sectors of the economy but have not achieved parity in the business world. Greece currently has three powerful women in key governmental positions (Mrs. Angelopoulou-Daskalaki, the Athens 2004 President, Mayor Dora Bakoyanni of Athens, and Fofi Gennimata, the Governor of the Attica Region). Women are very well represented in the medical, legal and engineering professions.

10. *Comments.* Showing interest and knowledge in Greek architecture, mythology and history both ancient and modern will definitively open doors for you. Greece's population of 11.5 million has exploded in the last few years with immigrants from the neighboring Balkan countries and from states of the previous Soviet Union. With one of the lowest birth rates in Europe, the 1.5 million immigrants have been a blessing to help complete the infrastructure for the Athens 2004

Olympics. Greece has given both legal and illegal immigrants free education and health care. In general, the integration of these immigrants has occurred with fewer problems than anticipated.

Hungary

1. In the business world, punctuality is important.

2. First *names* cannot be used upon meeting but will be appropriate when you know each other. Traditionally, the surname is first followed by the given name. Most married women use their husband's surname and add the suffix *né*. So when a woman marries Dr. Kovács, she becomes Kovácsné. Use *titles* in spoken communication.

3. *Business cards* are exchanged upon meeting. Your title should be on your card.

4. In the business world, you *greet* with a firm handshake.

5. *Business dress code* for men is a dark suit, white shirt and tie. *Business dress code* for women is a suit or dress.

6. In a social setting, do not miss the opportunity to thank your Hungarian hosts for their warm and generous hospitality. "Cheers" is "*egészségére.*"

7. *Non-verbal communication.* Hungarians like people who are straightforward and natural. Eye contact is direct.

8. *Your speech.* To begin your speech in Hungarian, you can say "*Jó napot,*" which means "Good day."

   Greeting VIPs at the beginning of your speech is customary.

   Humor is appreciated by Hungarians who have used it to help them survive difficult times.

   Hungarians are generally tolerant and philosophic about sensitive issues.

   In Question and Answer sessions, expect your audience to pay close attention, ask questions and respond eagerly.

9. *Especially for women.* Hungarian women are well-educated and respected for their achievements in the professional world. They are

comfortable with power and responsibility, which they wield with intelligence, creativity and femininity.

10. *Comments.* Hungarians are expressive, sensitive people who are inordinately proud of the accomplishments of fellow Hungarians, including scientists Teller Ede (Edward Teller, atomic energy), Szent-györgyi Albert (vitamin C), Neumann János and Wiegner Jenös. Well-known musicians are Bartók Béla, Kodály Zoltán and Liszt Ferenc (Franz Liszt).

India

1. India is moving with the times. Being fashionably late is no longer fashionable.

2. First *names* are not used upon meeting. Western India is more informal.

3. *Business cards* are exchanged upon meeting. *Titles* are used in spoken communication and very important when dealing with government officials.

4. In the business world, men *greet* by shaking hands. Women greet each other by shaking hands or *"namaste,"* which is the traditional Indian greeting. To make the *namaste,* place your palms together at chest level and say namaste (nah-mas-tey). Although foreigners are not expected to greet this way, Ted Habib of Compare Travel says, "Why not honor our custom of 'namaste.'" When men greet with *"namaste,"* they stand up straight. Men greeting women add a little bow. Women greeting men or each other always bow gently at the same time. In India after asking "How are you?" it is customary to ask "How is your family?"

5. *Business dress code* for men is suit and tie. *Business dress code* for women is suit with long sleeves and modest skirt length or trousers suit. A *"salwar kurta"* (traditional Indian outfit for men) and a *"salwar kameez"* (a traditional for women) are also acceptable.

6. The serving of alcohol depends upon the host. Alcohol is forbidden for Muslims and for Sikhs. To make a *toast,* say

"cheers" or "for a mutually beneficial business partnership." If you receive a toast, say "Thank you" or repeat the toast.

7. *Non-verbal communication*. Indians like people who have a respectful manner. Direct eye contact is very important. Pointing is considered rude. Standing with hands on hips is considered an aggressive action. If Indians shake their heads when listening or responding to you, they are signaling "I am listening to you" not necessarily agreement.

8. *Your speech*. Since India has 18 official languages and 1650 dialects, it's best to stick to English.

   Greeting VIPs at the beginning of your speech is customary.

   Humor is appreciated; however avoid jokes about religion, women, sex, cows and red dots.

   Sensitive issues include scams in government transactions, politics in general, pollution, Pakistan, Kashmir, Muslims.

   During your speech, do not be surprised if your audience interrupts to ask questions or make a point.

   In your Question and Answer session, expect eager participation.

9. *Especially for women*. In India, you will be treated with respect, but activities acceptable in the West like having a drink on your own or smoking in public may still be frowned upon. The rule for women, especially those traveling alone, is to blend in and act like the others. Your clothing should be tasteful, your manner subdued, but it is good to exude confidence. Most of all, smile. Indians love people who smile.

10. *Comments*. You will rarely get a definitive answer to a question. Be aware of the immense variety within India including many languages and seven major religions (Hinduism, Islam, Christianity, Sikhism, Buddhism, Zoroastrianism and Jainism.). Indians on the whole are well-educated and have a broad general knowledge in addition to their area of expertise, which makes them an appreciative and responsive audience. If you have difficulties understanding them, mention it kindly and they will slow down.

Indonesia

1. For meetings with government ministers and state-owned businesses, come fifteen minutes early. Although they may be late, they appreciate your arriving on *time*. For other business meetings, being five minutes late is tolerable. For social gatherings, time is very flexible.

2. Rank and status are important in Indonesia. If someone has *a title*, use it. Otherwise, for men use *Pak* (Mr.) or *Bapak* (Sir) with first name. A woman is addressed as *Ibu* with first name. You will be called Mr. or Mrs. with your first name.

3. *Business cards* are exchanged formally, as in Japan. Take time to read the card. Do not write on it. During a meeting, keep the card on the table in front of you.

4. In the business world, men *greet* by shaking hands. A woman should not initiate shaking hands; however if the man extends his hand, accept it graciously.

5. *Business dress code* for men is a long-sleeved light-colored shirt and tie with dark trousers, usually gray. Brown is seldom seen. Jackets are not worn. An invitation that says "lounge suit" requires a dark business suit.

   Business dress code for women is conservative in style and color. Upper arms must always be covered and skirt length must be modest. As Ines Sukandar says, "When I am meeting with the president of my company I wear a skirt and stockings to show respect."

6. To make a *toast*, say "to your health." If you receive a toast, say "thank you."

7. *Non-verbal communication.* Never point or give anyone something with your left hand, especially to someone older. Eye contact is direct.

8. *Your speech.* You might want to begin by saying *"Selamat Pagi," "Selamat Siang"* or *"Salamat Malan"* (good morning, good afternoon, good evening).

   Greeting VIPS at the beginning of your speech is crucial. Use their full title and name.

Humor: Indonesians are individualists and like to be humorous and even provocative in their own talks. Letting your personality shine through is highly acceptable, as long as it is not at the expense of others.

Politics, sex and religion are sensitive issues. Do not be overtly Christian. Indonesia has the world's largest Muslim population.

Some audiences will be polite—even if they are not impressed. Others will be livelier. Accepting phone calls during talks and meetings is common.

Question & Answer session: For the most part Indonesians are gregarious and like to debate. They will relish the chance to voice their opinions unless they fear they are exposing themselves to ridicule.

9. *Especially for women.* Having lunch with one man is accepted. Having dinner with one man might be misinterpreted. Drinking a cocktail or glass of wine is all right.

10. *Comments.* The Indonesians you will have dealings with are generally well-educated and proud of the cultural heritage. Their professionalism will vary greatly, however, as will their performance (in a job or in a speech.) Indonesians are extremely diverse, more so than in many Asian countries. They appreciate creative people and ideas and do not particularly cherish the ordinary.

Iran

1. While it is not uncommon for Iranians to be late for social gatherings (in fact it is fashionable), you are expected to be on *time* for meetings. Before getting down to business, spend some time in small talk, asking "How are you? And your family?"

2. First *names* are not used in the business world, or with neighbors or friends. You use *"Agha"* (Mr.) and *"Khanum"* (Mrs. or Ms.). *Titles* are used, especially for doctors and engineers. Titles are used quite freely so you might even call the employee of a pharmacy *"Aghayeh Doctor"* (Mr. Doctor).

3. *Business cards* are usually exchanged at the end of a meeting. Although business people print cards, they may forget to carry them. It is not rude to say, "I have run out of cards and will send you one."

4. In the business world, men shake hands with men; shaking hands between men and women is not permitted. As a woman, do not offer to shake hands with a man. After shaking hands, some men put their right hand on their chest. This gesture is also used for saying good-bye from a distance without shaking hands.

5. *Business dress* for a man is a suit without tie. When Khomeni came to power, he banned neckties as being Western. Nowadays, your host may wear a tie. Carry one in your pocket that you can put on when appropriate. Islam requires long sleeves for men. Business women must *dress* conservatively making sure they are well-covered. In Tehran, a scarf around the head and long, loose clothing is appropriate, preferably a semi-long coat with trousers underneath. Some younger women are wearing make-up in moderation. When visiting the provinces, especially religious sites, a chador is necessary.

6. No alcohol is consumed in Iran.

7. *Non-verbal communication.* Having your back to someone is very rude. It is appropriate to apologize even when it is unavoidable, for example, when you are waiting in a line or in an elevator. Do not use the left hand to pass things. The soles of your shoes should not point to anyone. Crossing your legs is not acceptable for women.

8. *Your speech.* Religious and official people begin by saying, *"Besmellah-e-rahman-rahim"* which means "in the name of God the merciful." This implies they are part of the post-revolutionary fabric of Iranian society, but foreigners are not expected to begin with this phrase.

   Greeting VIPs is very important at the beginning of your speech.

   Humor is well received.

   Sensitive issues include politics and religion. Avoid topics or jokes with sexual innuendoes.

   Especially when the speaker is not Iranian, the audience will be very attentive. It is rare and rude to disrupt a speech by intentional chatter. However, as elsewhere it is the speaker's responsibility to have the charisma and eye contact to keep people attentive.

During the Q&A, people will talk to each other. It is not impolite to request the audience to give everyone a chance to be heard. Do not be surprised to hear irrelevant questions.

9. *Especially for women.* Foreign women must remember the dress code and wear make-up in moderation. Iranian women are making strides and are eager to meet with women from other countries. The 2003 Nobel Peace Prize recipient is an Iranian woman who received this award for her work as a human rights activist and feminist lawyer.

10. *Comments.* Known until the 1930's as Persia, the modern official name is the Islamic Republic of Iran. Nowadays Persians look up to foreigners, but they will dismiss you quickly if they find your behavior even slightly insulting or disrespectful. An extra dose of visible respect in words, deeds and body language will reap rewards.

In 2003 the Nobel Peace Prize was awarded to Shirin Ebadi, lawyer, lecturer, writer, former judge and now the first Muslim woman and the first Iranian to receive this honor. Dr. Ebadi said, "It is very good for me, very good for human rights in Iran, good for democracy in Iran and especially children's rights in Iran."

Ireland

1. *Time* is becoming more respected.

2. First *names* are used upon meeting. *Titles* are not used in spoken communication.

3. *Business cards* are exchanged upon meeting.

4. In the business world, shake hands firmly, but not robustly.

5. *Business dress code* for men is suit and tie. Change to casual jacket and tie for less formal. *Business dress code* for women is a suit with skirt or trousers.

6. To make a *toast,* say "*Sláinte,*" which means "Health" in Gaelic. If you receive a toast, say "*Sláinte.*" Pronounced "Slauwn-Cha."

7. *Non-verbal communication*. Irish like people who are outgoing and confident. Eye contact is direct and a part of good communication.

8. *Your speech*. Best to stick to English as Gaelic albeit a beautiful language is difficult. However, you might try using the odd well-chosen Irish word in your speech. For example, *"craic"* (pronounced "crack") which is the wonderful entertainment only found in an Irish bar, as in "we had great crack last night."

   Greeting VIPs when you begin speaking is customary.

   The Irish are very good at telling jokes about themselves but they do not appreciate others telling jokes about them. It is better not to repeat the "Kerryman" joke you heard in the bar last night unless you know your audience very well.

   Sensitive issues include religion, divorce, abortion. As a foreigner, do not refer to Ireland as Eire. When someone says they are from Ireland, do not ask "North or South?" (They are from the South, i.e., the Republic.)

   During your speech, do not be surprised if your audience interrupts and asks questions. In a Question and Answer session, expect eager participation.

9. *Especially for women*. Provided you present yourself properly and "act the part," you will be received well in Ireland. There are many prominent women in politics, academia and business.

10. *Comments*. An Irish audience can cope with some theatricality but will expect a professional, thoughtful presentation rather than just a performance. The Irish education system is broadly based so Irish people tend to be well read. Literary quotes are well accepted, especially from one of their lesser known authors if you mention where in Ireland the writer comes from. Demonstrate your understanding of Ireland as a vibrant modern European country by being aware of key business, literary and political figures. The Irish love to have their country lauded in any way, saying, for example how much you enjoy "dapping in the Corrib."

Israel

1. *Time* is respected.

2. First *names* are used upon meeting. *Titles* are only used when you address an audience.

3. *Business cards* are not exchanged at any particular time. Translating your card into Hebrew on one side is not necessary but would be a nice gesture.

4. In the business world, *greeting* is by shaking hands before you meet in an office. Otherwise just say *"shalom."*

5. *Business dress code* for men: Speakers should be dressed in a business suit but expect a mixed appearance in your audience. *Business dress code* for women is also a suit. Banking has the most formal dress code, with computer and manufacturing industries at the other extreme.

6. Alcohol is consumed in moderation in Israel, and *toasts* are informal. To make a toast, say *"lecha'im"* (to life). If you receive a toast, you should respond by raising your glass and answering *"lecha'im."*

7. *Non-verbal communication.* Israelis like people who have an outgoing and confident manner. Eye contact is direct. Gestures to avoid include pointing. It is rude to cross your legs while seated and show the sole of your shoe.

8. *Your speech.* To begin in Hebrew, say *"Shalom"* (greetings) or *"Boker tov"* (good morning).

   Greeting VIPs at the beginning of your speech is customary.

   Humor is much appreciated if it is witty.

   Sensitive issues include Israeli politics, religion and the Israeli-Arab relationship.

   During your speech, do not be surprised if the audience talks to each other or if cell phones are not turned off.

   In a Question and Answer session, you may encounter limited participation. Even though many Israelis understand English, they are shy about making mistakes in public.

9. *Especially for women.* Business women from abroad are well-accepted in Israel. As a sign of respect, you should dress modestly with your arms and shoulders covered. Do not extend your hand to a man but wait and see if he offers to shake hands.

10. *Comments.* Israel is a very open society and this is reflected in the business code. Israelis are tough negotiators and eager to get the better of you. They will respect you for bargaining and holding your ground so expect to "horse-trade" and haggle. Do not expect to hear "please" or "thank you." Israelis are direct, interrupt and may sound angry when they are not. This should not be seen as impoliteness but as a compliment that you are being treated the way they treat other Israelis. Try to learn about biblical events associated with different places in the country and understand the current political and cultural problems, including unemployment and friction among different immigrant groups. As one Israeli said, "Unique problems create unique people."

Italy

1. In business, punctuality is highly appreciated.

2. First *names* cannot be used upon meeting. Ninety percent of Italians in business have degrees with *titles*, which are normally used in spoken communication, especially Dottore, Avvocato, Ingegnere and Professore. As in other countries, this is more relaxed with younger people.

3. *Business cards* are exchanged at no set time.

4. In the business world, you *greet* by shaking hands.

5. *Business dress code* for men is suit and tie. *Business dress code* for women is suit or trouser suit. Italians are fashion conscious and dress with taste and flair. They will expect you to wear stylish shoes, naturally!

6. To make a *toast*, say "*Alla salute di ...,*" "*salute,*" or "*cin cin*" (more colloquial). There is no set protocol to respond to a toast. Just raise your glass.

7. *Non-verbal communication.* Italians like people who have an informal manner. Eye contact is direct.

8. *Your speech.* Only use Italian if you feel completely confident. To begin in Italian: *"Buon giorno, signore e signori"* (Hello, ladies and gentlemen). *"E' un piacere essere qui in/a ..."* (It is a pleasure to be here in ...).

   Greeting VIPs at the beginning of your speech is customary.

   Italians do not have a great sense of humor when it comes to business. Do not overdo humor or be surprised if your attempts fall flat.

   Sensitive issues are politics, differences between the north and south and the Mafia.

   During your speech, do not be surprised if your audience talks to each other.

   In your Question and Answer session, expect limited participation.

9. *Especially for women.* An American business woman commented, "During meetings, you will be treated as a business woman. At a dinner, you will be treated as a woman. Enjoy it. Being aggressive will prove counterproductive."

10. *Comments.* Translating your presentation slides into Italian is a good idea and a necessity when you are addressing older people or the public sector. Italians will listen with interest if you take a pragmatic and personal approach, for example, saying, "I know because I have done it," or "It works because I have seen it with my own eyes." They are quick to understand, so stick to the point. Do not preach or inundate them with statistics and data.

Japan

1. Punctuality is very important. In private situations, there may be a five-minute delay.

2. First *names* are not used. The order is surname first, given name second. In speaking, use the surname followed by 'san' which corresponds to 'Mr.' or 'Mrs.' For example: Yamasaki-san. Younger people use first names among friends and "family name + san" profession-

ally and with older people. *Titles* are normally used in spoken communication.

3. *Business cards* are exchanged immediately. Translating your card into Japanese is appreciated. Use the same quality of print on both sides and include your title. Ask a Japanese friend to ensure an accurate translation. Japanese businesspeople tend to separate outsiders. When they see a poor Japanese business card, they regard the visitor as an outsider. Present your business card with both hands, showing the Japanese side with name towards your counterpart. When you receive a card, take it with both hands and look at it respectfully. Refrain from writing on it. Put it away carefully. Business cards received at a meeting may be placed on the table in front of you (in order of where the respective people are sitting) to help remember names and to refer to them by name during the meeting. You need a special holder for cards; do not keep them in your wallet or pocket.

4. In the business world, the Japanese bow to each other. When bowing, keep your back straight. The more important the person is who you are bowing to, the lower and longer the bow. Do not try to out bow a Japanese, however a polite nod is appreciated. Japanese may shake hands with you, but their grip may not be firm and they may avert their eyes.

5. *Business dress code* for men is conservative. Dark suits, white shirts, subdued ties. Software engineers don't wear suits.

   Business dress code for women is conservative. Wear neutral colors, long sleeves, and modest length skirts. Tailored trousers and short skirts are becoming accepted. Stockings are a must. Keep jewelry and perfume to a minimum.

6. To make a *toast*, say 'Kan pai.'

   To reply, say 'Kan pai.'

7. *Non-verbal communication*. Japanese like people who are respectful and deferential. You are expected to keep your emotions to yourself. Eye contact may be direct or indirect. Be aware that even when Japanese try to make direct eye contact, they may feel uncomfortable. Gestures must be used with caution. If you need to indicate some-

thing, wave with your palm up. To beckon, wave with your palm down.

8. *Your speech.* To begin in Japanese, good morning is '*ohayo gozaimasu*' and good afternoon is '*konnichiwa.*' Then it is polite to say, "As you already have learned from Mr. X (the person who introduced you), my name is John Smith. It is a great privilege for me to be addressing you today and you give me great honor with your presence."

   Greeting VIPs is very important, beginning with the person of highest rank.

   Use humor with restraint. Everyone is attending for a serious purpose. Humor is all right during your Question and Answer session.

   Sensitive issues include the Imperial family, WWII, forced prostitution, and mentioning of the minority group of Buraku. Other issues are the so-called "three-Ss": Politics (*Seiji*), religion (*Syukyo*), and sex (Sex).

   During your speech, do not be surprised if some in your audience close their eyes to listen.

   In your Question and Answer session, expect limited participation. If you feel someone is reflecting on what you have said, allow the prolonged silence to give them adequate time to think—their responses will be more meaningful to you. Some Japanese prefer to ask questions individually after the session.

   At the end, the phrase '*yoroshiku onegai shimasu*' is customary for negotiation-type speeches or at discussion in a small group. It means 'please stay favorably inclined to me.' At the end of your speech say "*doomo arigatoo gozaimashita*" which means "thank you."

9. *Especially for women.* In Japan, women appear to have a lower status than men; however, this is a role they are required to play and does not mirror their esteem or status in private life. Today there are strong women's associations, and women are important in business and politics. Foreign business women will be well accepted in the business world. They can opt out of visits to Karaoke bars without any business repercussions whereas their foreign male colleagues have to join in.

10. *Comments.* Language can cause many misunderstandings. If you say, "Can we meet tomorrow?" and the Japanese says, "That would be difficult," he may mean, "I do not want to meet with you." You must become sensitive to what is being implied. Japanese strive to maintain harmony at all costs. Patience is very important. At a personal level however, it is more direct. If someone says, "It is difficult," it means, "I want to try but can't cannot commit right now." Do not try to be too Japanese. Japanese people do not appreciate foreigners who are too much at ease. They take pride in being different.

Jordan

1. Although *time* is flexible among Arabs, a Westerner will be treated according to his or her customs with which Jordanians are very familiar, so play it safe and be punctual.

2. First *names* can be used. However, in polite conversation, the whole name is used. Titles can also be used. "*Ustad*" (Mr. or Sir), "*Brofessor*" ("Professor") and "Doctor".

3. *Business cards* are exchanged at the end of a meeting.

4. In the business world, men shake hands. A man may not touch any woman other than his wife so he will not offer to shake hands with a woman. It is best for a woman to put her hand over her heart and nod while greeting a man. Then the man will mirror the gesture with his hand over his heart.

5. Western *business dress code* of dark suit and tie is acceptable for men. Women need to be well-tailored with modest necklines and hemlines and no upper arm showing. Shoes should be very conservative. Arabs know good leather, and you will be judged by your shoes.

6. Alcohol is rare so there is no toasting. When *toasts* are made, they are Western style. It is best to skip them.

7. *Non-verbal communication.* Do not show the bottom of your shoe to any one; it means you consider them beneath you. The "OK" hand signal is very obscene in Jordan.

8. *Your speech.* You may start your speech with *"B'esm'illáh ir-rahhmán ir-rahím."* (In the Name of God, the Merciful, the Compassionate) but only if it can be said with strength and dignity.

   VIPs are introduced in the beginning. You do not thank them for coming, however. You thank God for allowing them to come.

   Humor can be attempted if it is relaxing and community-building. However, a little wry humor or gently self-deprecating humor is sufficient. If your audience thinks you are a fool you are dead in the water. A woman needs to be extra careful about this. Laughter is considered to be flirtatious.

   Sensitive issues include politics, royalty, government, Israel. Men never ask about the women in another man's family. Never mention women—how they act, dress, speak. (even if you are a woman.) A woman never mentions a man's appearance or behavior.

   During your speech, your audience will listen and will comment to each other *soto voce* when you have touched them in some way, good or bad.

   Jordanians love a good Q&A session and will ask penetrating and challenging questions. They love logical reasoning in an answer, too.

9. *Especially for women.* Dress conservatively. Keep eyes direct and serious.

   Be cautious about smiling too broadly or laughing out loud. Never flirt.

10. *Comments.* Therea Lepard Malloy advises to "be aware in speaking that the words 'air,' 'zip,' 'zipper,' 'kiss,' 'cuss' and 'maniac' closely resemble Arabic words for sexual organs and sexual acts. Speak in a well-modulated voice. Sometimes Arabs will get quite loud, but a Westerner should not."

    When doing business in Jordan, remember the importance of hospitality. A host will do anything to make sure his guests are comfortable. He would never allow sorrow or harm to come to his guests as that would bring him great shame. If a business meeting reaches an undesirable ending, the news will be delivered gently on a different day, in a different place, preferably when the guest has reached his or her own home.

Lithuania

1. *Time* is fixed.

2. First names are not used upon meeting. *"Ponas"* for Mr. and *"Ponia"* for Mrs. or Ms. *Titles* are used with last name. Doctors and teachers are addressed by their title alone.

3. *Business cards* are exchanged at the beginning of a meeting.

4. In the business world, you *greet* by shaking hands. Take care not to do this over a door step which is considered bad luck.

5. *Dress code* is the general European standard. *Business dress code* for men is a suit and tie. For women, a suit or skirt with blouse.

6. To make a *toast* say *"I sveikata"* which is "to your health".

7. *Non-verbal communication.* Eye contact is direct, especially when greeting someone or proposing a toast.

8. *Your speech.* Start your speech with *"Gerbiamos Ponios ir Ponai ..."* which means "Dear Ladies and Gentlemen."

   Avoid discussing politics.

   Expect your audience to be quite reserved. It is uncommon for Lithuanians to loudly express themselves.

9. *Especially for women.* You will be accepted in Lithuania.

10. *Comments.* Lithuania is the largest of the Balkan States. It has been occupied by Germans, Russians and Poles. In 1944 the Soviets incorporated Lithuania in the USSR; however, the Lithuanians never gave up their goal to be independent. This was finally achieved in 1991. The Lithuanians have a strong national identity. Avoid mixing them up with Latvians or Estonians.

Malaysia

1. *Time* is "respectfully flexible."

2. Protocol is extremely important. Using *names* and *titles*

correctly is a great asset. First names are not used upon meeting. (You will probably be called by Mr. or Mrs. with your first name.) Titles such as Doctor, Engineer and Professor are used with surnames. There are several levels in society:

- *"Tengku"* is Prince and notes a royal connection.

- *"Tan Sri"* is similar to Lord and is generally bestowed upon people who have made a mark in business or society. *"Puan Sri"* is the female equivalent. These titles are used on their own.

- *"Dato"* is a similar title which can be bestowed upon a man or a woman. The wife of a "Dato" is referred to as *"Datin"*. This does not work in reverse.

3. *Business cards* are exchanged upon meeting.

4. In the business world, you *greet* by shaking hands firmly. Business women also shake hands, although not firmly. Malays may shake with both hands.

5. Because the climate is very warm, *business dress code* for men may be a long-sleeved shirt and tie or Batik shirt, which is a lightweight colorfully printed Malaysian fabric. It is appreciated when foreigners wear Batik because it is seen as embracing the local culture. Jackets are only expected at big official meetings. "Lounge suit" means dark business suit. *Business dress code* for women is conservative. Dresses are popular. Your upper arms should be covered and your skirt length modest. Malaysian women always wear long clothes, often Batik. Western women must remember the dominant religion is Muslin. Do not wear yellow on formal occasions as this color is reserved for the king.

6. To make a *toast*, say a few words of appreciation. To respond, offer a toast in return.

7. *Non-verbal communication.* Eye contact can be direct. Malays like people who have a respectful and quiet manner. They are not confrontational and will rarely give you an outright "no" so you must be very observant of body language. The people you meet with in the early stages are not the decision makers so you must work to help them support your proposals with their superiors.

8. *Your speech*. Greeting VIPs at the beginning of your speech is customary.

Humor is appreciated if it is witty.

Sensitive issues include race, religion and local politics. Be aware that the media is pro-Islamic. There is rising opposition against the US. Even Chinese Malaysians have an anti-Western and especially anti-American point of view. Malays are emotional and discussing the Western-Islamic conflict needs to be done with great tact.

During your speech, do not be surprised if some people in the audience leave occasionally, especially to take a phone call.

In your Question and Answer session, expect limited participation.

9. *Especially for women*. Women are not expected to come across forcefully. Smoking in public is frowned upon.

10. *Comments*. The term "Malaysian" refers to all the citizens of Malaysia. The term "Malay" refers to the largest ethnic group in Malaysia.

Malays use the given name followed by father's name, for example, Samad bin Abdullah. Samad is the given name, *bin* means "son of" (*binti* means "daughter of") and Abdullah is the father's name. You address him as "*Encik Samad*," which means Mr. Samad. You use Samad on a first-name basis. (*Puan* means "Mrs." and *Cik* means "Miss.")

Chinese start with the family name, followed by the first names, for example, Lim Chin Kok where Lim is the family name. Address him as Mr. Lim or Chin Kok if on a first name basis.

Indians use the given name, followed by father's name, for example, Saji Raghavan where Saji is the given name and Raghavan is the father's name. Address him as Mr. Saji or Saji on a first-name basis. As mentioned above, you will probably be called "Mr." or "Mrs." with your first name which is easier for them and for you to remember!

Mexico

1. *Time* is sacred when meeting a senior person. Socially, time is flexible.

2. First *names* are not used upon first meeting. A person may have two surnames, the father's and the mother's first surname. When talking with someone, the father's name is used. In spoken communication, people like to be addressed with their *titles*. For example, Licenciado Doctor with surname or simply Doctor.

3. *Business cards* are exchanged upon meeting or at the end of an interview.

4. In the business world, men and women usually *greet* by shaking hands. Women generally exchange warm smiles with the handshake. In a group, first greet the women or the senior people.

5. *Business dress code* for men is a suit and tie. Conservative ties are better. *Business dress code* for women is a suit. (No miniskirts.) Trouser suits are also acceptable, but skirts or trousers should not be tight. Depending on the occasion, a suit with short sleeves or a dress in light colors is fine.

6. To make a *toast*, say "I would like to wish Mr. Perez great professional success." To respond to a toast, say "Thank you for your kind words." In Mexico, "cheers" is "*Salud.*"

7. *Non-verbal communication*. Eye contact can be direct but should not be too long or insistent. Avoid pointing to a person or being too effusive in business.

8. *Your speech*. Opening remarks in Spanish: "*Buenos dias/buenas tardes, señoras y señores.*" "*Es un placer estar aqui con Ustedes.*"

Make sure you are introduced properly and with due credit.

Greeting VIPs at the beginning of your speech is necessary.

Humor is appreciated if it is subtle. Never tell double-entendre jokes if women are present.

Sensitive issues include the Mexican-American border and the economy. Avoid speaking about politics (unless the meeting is a political one), religion or money. During your speech, do not be surprised if some people within your audience leave occasionally.

In your Question and Answer session, expect limited participation. However, be prepared to establish a time limit to deal with people who may try to expose their ideas instead of asking pertinent questions.

9. *Especially for women*. If you are the speaker, elegance and simplicity are the key words. Always wear stockings and closed shoes. Apply at least light make-up and be sure that your hair is neat looking. Keep accessories to a minimum.

10. *Comments*. Showing respect for your audience is fundamental if you want to be well received. When referring to Mexico, it helps to express the wish for improvement in the current situation instead of only mentioning the problems facing the country.

The Netherlands

1. *Time* is respected.

2. First *names* may be used upon meeting. *Titles* are not normally used in spoken communication, except for political titles and medical doctors.

3. *Business cards* are exchanged when you meet or say goodbye.

4. In the business world, you *greet* by shaking hands. Once you know someone, you may greet by kissing three times when you come from south of the rivers where people are predominantly Catholic. Twice in the north where people are predominantly Protestant!

5. *Business dress code* for men is suit or jacket with tie. *Business dress code* for women is well-tailored suit or trouser suit — stylish but not power dressing. As in many western countries, dress codes are relaxing, however, you won't go wrong if you stick to dark and neutral colors.

6. To make a *toast*, you can say a few words and end with "*Proost*" or "to your health." If you receive a toast, nod graciously and say thank you.

7. *Non-verbal communication.* The Dutch like people who have an informal and forthright manner. Eye contact is direct.

8. *Your speech.* There is no typical way to begin a speech. Feel free to start with *"Goedemorgen/Goedemiddag, dames en heren."* (Good morning/good afternoon, ladies and gentlemen.) *"Het is een genoegen hier in ... te zijn."* (It's a pleasure to be here in . . .)

   Greeting VIPs when you begin speaking is customary.

   Humor is appreciated but avoid jokes about racism and homosexuality.

   Sensitive issues include racism, WW II, religion and legalized prostitution.

   During your speech, do not be surprised if your audience asks questions.

   In your Question and Answer session, expect participation, however, do not be put off by direct, even blunt questions. When Dutch people want to know something, they will ask!

   At a staff meeting in New York, Hanneke C. Frese (Dutch citizen) asked, "May I say this to you in Dutch?" as a constructive and fun way to be open and honest. Before long this phrase was used in her firm from Sri Lanka to Los Angeles. At one global conference a senior American stood up and asked the Swiss CEO, "May I ask you something in Dutch?" "Fine," replied the CEO, "and my answer will be in Dutch, too."

   As Hanneke says, "When we 'speak Dutch,' we alert our colleagues that what we are saying is important and apologize upfront that the phrasing may not be elegant."

9. *Especially for women.* You will be well accepted and will find that Dutch women are very much part of the work force juggling their careers and families with aplomb.

10. *Comments.* The Dutch are open and direct, even aggressive. You may find their humor very broad. They are excellent linguists and very good business people. They are not impressed by people who brag about their salary or jobs. Also remember that "Holland" makes up a portion of the Netherlands so it is incorrect to refer to the entire coun-

try by that name. A typical Dutch lunch may consist of a sandwich and buttermilk, which is normal fare for CEO to the mailroom clerk. Do not be offended if you are served this for lunch.

New Zealand

1. *Time* is respected.

2. You can use first *names* upon meeting. *Titles* are not used in spoken communication, except for Professor and medical Doctor.

3. *Business cards* are exchanged when you meet in no set fashion.

4. In the business world, you *greet* by shaking hands.

5. *Business dress code* for men is suit or jacket and tie. *Business dress code* for women is suit or trouser suit. Stockings.

6. Making and responding to *toasts* is quite informal. You can say, "I would like to propose a toast ..." To respond, say a few words.

7. *Non-verbal communication.* New Zealanders like people who are informal. Eye contact is direct. Don't stand too close.

8. *Your speech.* Greeting VIPs when you begin speaking is customary.

   Humor is appreciated if it is witty, but avoid jokes about gender or sheep.

   Sensitive issues include abortion, Asian immigration, race relations, women.

   During your speech, do not be surprised if your audience leaves mobile phones on.

   In your Question and Answer session, expect limited participation.

9. *Especially for women.* An Australian woman put it this way: "American women are more 'in your face' than we Australians are, but we're more assertive than New Zealand women. So depending on where you are coming from, you may have to adapt."

10. *Comments.* New Zealanders are real team players. They are not good at self-promotion. They love being complimented about their beautiful country and their great wine.

Norway

1. *Time* is respected.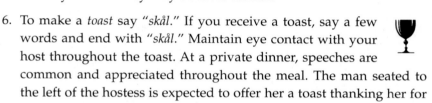

2. First *names* are not used when you first meet. You need to know each other a little. *Titles* are not normally used in spoken communication.

3. *Business cards* are usually exchanged upon meeting.

4. In the business world, you *greet* by shaking hands.

5. *Business dress code* for men is a suit or jacket with tie. *Business dress code* for women is a suit or trouser suit. Norwegians are not overly concerned with the latest fashions and dress quite casually. In Oslo they may be more formal.

6. To make a *toast* say "*skål*." If you receive a toast, say a few words and end with "*skål*." Maintain eye contact with your host throughout the toast. At a private dinner, speeches are common and appreciated throughout the meal. The man seated to the left of the hostess is expected to offer her a toast thanking her for the lovely meal and hospitality.

7. *Non-verbal communication*. Norwegians like people who have an informal manner. Eye contact is direct. Norwegians like their space. No hugging or kissing when greeting, although this is changing with the younger generation.

8. *Your speech*. Opening in Norwegian: "*God Dag*" ("Good day" can be used morning and afternoon). "*Det er hyggelig å vaere her*" (It is a pleasure to be here).

Greeting VIPs when you begin speaking is customary.

Humor is fine but avoid jokes about whale hunting or Greenpeace.

Sensitive issues. Because Norway is a homogenous society, the extreme positions in politics are much closer than in other European countries. Although 90 percent belong to the state church, mentioning religion is considered a personal intrusion.

During your speech, do not be surprised if your audience asks questions. In your Question & Answer session, expect limited participation.

Norwegians do not easily show their feelings or give compliments, so do not expect much positive feedback from your speech.

9. *Especially for women.* Ever since Viking men started going off to sea, Norway has been ably managed by women. They are active members of society and often found at the speaker's lectern. The women's liberation movement began in the 1970s. Men do not cater to women or treat them in a cavalier fashion, but as equals. Gro Harlem Brundtland, a highly respected Norwegian who served as Prime Minister and then took over as Director-General of the World Health Organization in 1998, has done much to open the door for women around the world.

10. *Comments.* Norwegians are patriotic and proud of their orderly and well-run country with its solid economic status. They find it difficult to imagine living anywhere else. They might not understand your point of view if it doesn't acknowledge the superiority of the social democratic system of government. They share many fundamental values and are unused to the differences which exist elsewhere, which makes them sensitive to criticism.

Pakistan

1. *Time.* In multinational settings, people are punctual. If you have a one-to-one meeting with a minister, it is important to be on time. However, expect delays. If someone says a meeting will start at 2 p.m., don't be surprised to wait.

2. At a formal meeting, use titles with surnames. Age and position are important. Do not address your counterparts by first names unless invited to do so.

3. *Business cards* are exchanged at the beginning of a meeting as each person is introduced.

4. *Greeting.* When men meet, it is perfectly acceptable to shake hands. Either party may initiate. However, foreign men should not extend their hand to women. A polite smile and nod will suffice.

5. *Dress code* for men: During business meetings, either light or dark suit is fine during the day. Except for formal meetings

with high level government officials or senior executives, a long-sleeved shirt and tie is also acceptable, especially during the summer months. Dark suits are preferable for evening events.

Business dress for women is conservative. Women may wear trousers which are not form-fitting. Long-sleeved jackets or blouses are a must. The blouse may be accompanied by a silk scarf during the day or a pashmina shawl in the evening, especially in the winter months. The scarf or shawl will come in handy to cover the woman's hair when visiting mosques and religious shrines.

6. *Toasts* are not common as alcohol is not consumed except in five-star hotels. Your host may offer a non-alcoholic toast at a formal banquet so be prepared to respond by showing your appreciation.

7. *Non-verbal communication.* Pakistanis are fairly direct in their dialogue. Eye contact is permissible between men but is impolite when addressing women.

8. *Your speech.* Greeting VIPs at the beginning of your speech is customary. Always use titles. For example, His Excellency, Mr. (surname), the Governor of Sindh.

   Humor is acceptable, especially if something goes awry. Avoid political and religious themes.

   Sensitive issues include politics, religion and the military. Avoid discussions about the relationship with India.

   Audience reaction and participation is encouraged, especially at conferences.

   Question and Answer sessions are widely used, especially in academia. Set a time limit or limit the number of questions. Have your host moderate, if possible.

9. *Especially for women.* Women should always dress conservatively. Do not offer to shake hands with your hosts or guests, but do accept a handshake if offered. Try to avoid sustained eye contact with male members of your audience. Avoid using first names. Avoid flashy jewelry and make-up. In rural areas, women should avoid traveling alone or with a man who is not a relative. It is inadvisable to shop

alone except in the arcades of major hotels. Pakistanis are hospitable and will gladly arrange for you to be escorted on a shopping trip or outing by a female staff member or perhaps the wife of your host.

10. *Comments*. Many Pakistanis in urban areas have strong Western backgrounds and tend to accept minor faux pas made by foreigners.

The Philippines

1. *Time* is flexible.

2. First *names* cannot be used upon meeting. *Titles* are used in spoken communication, especially Doctor and Professor and other professionals (engineer, architect.)

3. *Business cards* are exchanged upon meeting. Take the card with both hands and read the card carefully before placing it on the table during your meeting.

4. In the business world, you greet by shaking hands. You also shake hands at the end of meetings.

5. *Business dress code* for men is dark suit and tie or barong tagalog, the traditional embroidered shirt which is worn outside dark trousers. The short-sleeved version is for everyday business wear. For formal occasions, the long-sleeved version is better. To appear distinguished, wear the natural pineapple cloth barong. Underneath you wear a plain white round neck T-shirt. *Business dress code* for women is a suit with skirt below the knees or trouser suit. Avoid bright or neon colors. Knit twin sets are acceptable. Sleeveless blouses should always be worn with a sweater or jacket.

6. To make a *toast*, say "Cheers!" If you receive a toast, say "Thank you."

7. *Non-verbal communication*. Filipinos like people who have a respectful manner. They themselves are polite. Eye contact is direct.

   Avoid crossing your arms or putting your hand on your chin.

8. *Your speech*. The official languages are English and Pilipino (which is a mixture of several languages: English, Spanish, Chinese and Malay).

Over 70 dialects are spoken. To begin in Pilipino: "*Magandang umaga* (good morning), *tanghali* (for a lunchtime speech), *hapon* (afternnoon) or *gabi* (evening). *nnno sa inyong lahat,* (ladies and gentlemen)".

"*Ikinagagalak kong makarating dito sa Maynila at makapiling kayong lahat sa pagtitipong ito*" (It is a pleasure to be in Manila and to be with you on this occasion).

Greeting VIPs at the beginning of your speech is necessary. Be sure you include all the VIPs.

Humor is appreciated, as are lively and entertaining speeches, but Filipinos would be very offended if you told a joke about the Pope.

Sensitive issues include religion and politics.

During your speech, do not be surprised if the audience talks to each other or leaves occasionally.

In your Question & Answer session, audiences are ready to participate.

Do not be offended if you receive minimal applause after your speech because most people are very reserved.

9. *Especially for women.* A speaking engagement is considered a formal occasion so choose your dress with care. Filipinos are number one critics in fashion. "Be simple, but beautiful enough." As a business woman, you probably will be treated differently because male chauvinism still exists, for example, having a drink at the hotel bar on your own is not accepted. Even proposing a toast at a business dinner would not be appropriate.

10. *Comments.* Filipinos are friendly and hospitable and will do their best to make you feel at home. As a foreign speaker, you will be treated with respect, but you must take care to avoid appearing arrogant. Filipinos hate a "high and mighty" approach. The audience needs to know that you are there to help them, not to conquer. Be friendly and approachable.

Poland

1. *Time* is highly valued in the private sector. Delays still happen, but punctuality signals that you mean business.

2. First *names* are not used upon meeting. In Polish, use "Pan" for "Mr." and "Pani" for "Mrs." with surname. Although there is a tradition of mentioning business titles, they are not as important as in countries like Germany. You are advised to concentrate on remembering names and pronouncing them correctly.

3. *Business cards* aren't exchanged in any set way. Your card should include your position. When you receive a card, do not put it away immediately.

4. In the business world, you greet by shaking hands. If a man kisses a woman's hand, she should graciously accept his old-world gallantry instead of getting upset.

5. *Business dress code* for men is suit or jacket and tie. *Business dress code* for women is suit or trouser suit. In the warmer months, short sleeves are acceptable.

6. To make a *toast* in Polish, if you mention something favorable about the history of Poland, people will admire your knowledge of their country which is rare among foreigners. Then you can say, *"na zdrowie"* ("cheers") or *"za dalsza wspolprace"* ("for further cooperation"). When you receive a toast, raise your glass and say *"dziekujje bardzo"* ("thank you very much"). Everyone will follow suit. Drinking your slivovitz (70 percent alcohol) like a man (straight, cold, no ice, bottoms up) will get you an ovation if you are man or woman.

7. *Non-verbal communication.* Poles like people who have an outgoing, easy manner. Even if they appear formal, they will warm up after the initial contact. Direct eye contact is essential. Otherwise, you will be thought to be hiding something.

8. *Your speech.* To begin your speech in Polish, say *"Dzien dobry panstwu"* ("Good morning, ladies and gentlemen"). This form is used throughout the day until evening when one says, *"Dobry wieczór panstwu."* *"Jest dla mnie ogromna przyjemnoscia ze moglem sie tu znalezc"* (It is a pleasure to be here).

Greeting VIPs at the beginning of your speech is absolutely necessary.

Polish people appreciate humor if it is free of puns, most of which do not translate.

Sensitive issues include communism, Jewish origin and sex.

Do not be surprised if your audience whispers among themselves a bit.

In your Question & Answer session, initial response may be meager. Poles are unaccustomed to expressing themselves openly, however this is changing rapidly.

Translating your slides and written materials into Polish will ensure good comprehension. Be sure to have everything proofread by a native speaker.

9. *Especially for women*. Poland has produced several senior leaders: a female prime minister, a female Minister of Construction and Spatial Planning, as well as an Ombudsman. Mentioning that fact never hurts. Business men will be more impressed by your command of the current economic and political situation than your wardrobe, although looking attractive will win you extra points.

10. *Comments*. If you weave a reference to Poland's cultural "golden days" into your speech, you will touch a chord. Rapid strides are being made, but Poland is aware of being considered poor in the eyes of Europe. You will also impress your audience if you can refer to recent quotes made by the Polish Minister of your industry. A valuable source for information is the Polish Agency of Foreign Investment (PAIZ). Finally, smile! When I began a talk in Warsaw with poem by Wislava Szymborska, winner of the Nobel Prize for Literature in 1996, the rapport with my audience was immediate and lasting.

Portugal

1. *Time* is respected.

2. First *names* cannot be used upon meeting. The order of names is given name, two family names: mother's and father's. Portuguese often choose which of their names they use because of personal preference or status. *Titles* such as Doutor, Engenheiro and Arquitecto (Doctor, Engineer and Architect) are used in spoken communication.

3. *Business cards* are exchanged when another meeting is foreseen.

4. In the business world, you *greet* by is by shaking hands. Women who know each other greet by kissing twice on the cheek, first on the right side.

5. *Business dress code* for men is a dark suit and tie in the winter and light suit and tie in the summer. *Business dress code* for women is a suit, trouser suit or a dress. The dress code is conservative and being well-dressed is important.

6. To make a *toast*, say a few words. Don't make a long speech. Reply with a short, formal but witty toast to the audience. Cheers is "*Saúde.*"

7. *Non-verbal communication.* To be accepted, people should have a respectful manner. Eye contact is direct.

8. *Your speech.* Opening: Good morning: "*bom dia,*" good afternoon: "*boa tardé,*" ladies and gentlemen: "*senhoras e senhores.*"

   "It's a pleasure to be here in ...": "*é um grande prazer estar aqui em ...*"

   Greeting VIPs at the beginning of your speech is customary.

   Humor is appreciated if it is witty.

   Sensitive issues; until 1974, Portugal was a dictatorship. Since then, freedom of speech is evident. However, it is best to avoid disparaging remarks about the Roman Catholic Church.

   During your speech, do not be surprised if your audience occasionally leaves or talks to each other.

   In your Question & Answer session, expect limited participation.

9. *Especially for women.* In the business world, women are well respected. If a man pays you a compliment, do not be surprised or offended. Portugal is a Latin country, where men still enjoy being charming to a woman.

10. *Comments.* Portuguese people would be impressed if you referred to their explorers like Vasco da Gama, who discovered the route to India, and Pedro Alvares Cabral, who first landed in Brazil.

Russia

1. *Time* is flexible. Patience is necessary.

2. First *names* are not used upon meeting. The order of names is given name, middle name, surname. For example: Alexander Petrovich Ivanov. Alexander is the given name; Petrovich is derived from the father's first name; Ivanov is the family name. Formally, you would say Mr. Ivanov. Younger people in business are adopting Western standards by eliminating the second name. Titles are not generally used in spoke communication.

3. *Business cards* are exchanged at the beginning of the meeting. Translating your business card into Russian is necessary.

4. In the business world, you greet by shaking hands. Usually a man initiates a handshake with a woman. As a man, do not be surprised if a Russian male hugs and kisses you (the "Russian bear hug") once you know each other. This is a sign of friendship often preceded by excessive vodka.

5. *Business dress code* for men is dark suit and tie. *Business dress code* for women is a conservative suit or trouser suit.

6. To make a *toast*, say *"Za vashe Zdorovje"* which means "to your health." If you receive a toast, reply by toasting to the health of your host or the success of your cooperation. Toasts are informal but a regular and frequent custom.

7. *Non-verbal communication.* Russians like people who have an informal manner. Eye contact is direct. Avoid pointing at your temple (meaning "you're an idiot").

8. *Your speech.* Beginning in Russian: Good morning/good evening, ladies and gentlemen: *"Dobroye utro/dobry vecher, damy i gospoda."* It's a pleasure to be here: *"Mne preyátno byts vámi zdes' v . . . ."*

   Greeting VIPs at the beginning of your speech is customary.

   Clever humor is appreciated but avoid jokes about individuals or specific groups of people.

   Sensitive issues are internal Russian politics, the army, NATO, corruption and the "Russian mafia."

   Translating your slides and written material into Russian is necessary.

   During your speech, do not be surprised if some in your audience seem to sleep, leave occasionally or talk to each other.

   In your Question & Answer session, expect limited participation.

9. *Especially for women.* You will be treated as a "real woman," i.e., with Eastern European courtesy. Having dinner or a drink at the hotel bar on your own is acceptable but not recommended. Women in Russian business still have to fight to be taken seriously. Long business dinners with sufficient vodka consumption doesn't make it easier for a woman. Nevertheless, do not hide your "feminine nature." Be natural: your charm will help you to build valuable relationships.

10. *Comments.* Business in Russia is very much influenced by relationships. Often negotiations and contract discussions are held during long relaxed dinners and sauna including vodka drinking as part of the program. When I organized a conference in St. Petersburg, my non-Russian speakers feared that if they consumed the mandatory amount of vodka at the pre-conference dinner, they would be incoherent the following morning. With their consent, I seated them together and filled their vodka bottles with water. They toasted until midnight and were in top form the following day.

Saudi Arabia

1. *Time* is flexible. Always be on time but expect to wait.

2. To address someone, use their last *name* with Mr. or Mrs. if

they do not have a title. *Titles* are definitely used. With Doctor or Professor, use the surname. With other titles use the given name, as you use with a member of British aristocracy, for example, Prince Saud (given name) or Sheikh Ali (given name) or simply Your Royal Highness or Your Excellency (Minister).

3. *Business cards* are exchanged upon meeting.

4. In the business world, men *greet* by shaking hands. As a woman, do not initiate shaking hands.

5. *Business dress code* for men is suit with tie. *Business code* for women is modest. Wear conservative, even loose fitting clothes with long sleeves and skirt below the knees. Nothing revealing.

6. Alcohol is not consumed so *toasts* do not exist. Never turn down an offer of coffee or tea.

7. *Non-verbal communication.* Eye contact is direct but not piercing. Sitting with your legs crossed so that the soles of your shoes are exposed is a great insult, as is pointing at someone.

8. *Your speech.* To begin in Arabic: "*Assalaamu Alaikum*" which means "Hello," or literally, "Peace be with you all."

   Greeting VIPs at the beginning of your speech is mandatory.

   Be very cautious in using humor.

   In your Question & Answer session, expect participation.

   Sensitive issues include politics, especially the monarchy v. democracy, women's rights, USA.

9. *Especially for women.* You need an invitation from the Saudi Arabian ministry in order to visit or work. Visas are granted on a case-by-case basis.

10. *Comments.* What you can do to really impress your audience is to use poetry or allusions to Islamic or Arabic history and literature. In Saudi Arabia, hospitality is important and as a guest you should show due appreciation. Although social conversation usually begins a meeting, it is inappropriate to ask about a Saudi's family unless you

already have met them. If you are invited to a private dinner, a prompt answer is expected. Always be courteous, for example, at a doorway always offer to let the other person (man or woman) go first. At prayer times, your audience may leave to pray. During Ramadan, do not expect to be served any food or drink during daylight hours.

Singapore

1. *Time* is respected.

2. Generally larger companies are switching to first names. You can ask people how they would like to be addressed and then have them address you with the same degree of formality. Be aware that Singapore's three major ethnic groups have different ways of ordering names. It shows respect to address senior people first.

3. *Business cards* are exchanged with two hands. Read the card carefully and show that you are impressed with the details.

4. In the business world, you greet by shaking hands or by smiling warmly; however, since the advent of SARS, some people have reverted to greeting by bowing slightly and clasping their hands together (as if praying) to avoid the handshake. In this case, keep your hands to yourself and be natural.

5. *Business dress code* for men is usually a light colored shirt and tie. For dinners and major meetings, a dark suit and tie is necessary.

   Business dress code for women is a dark or neutral colored suit. Stockings are optional.

6. To make a *toast*, say, "Here is to good success and future endeavors." If you receive a toast, you can respond by saying a few words.

7. *Non-verbal communication.* Singaporeans like people who are respectful and polite. It is courteous to keep a level of eye contact that shows sincerity. Gestures to avoid include pointing or standing with your arms crossed in front of you.

8. *Your speech.* It is best to stick to English because otherwise you would have to choose among English, Mandarin, Malay or Indian.

   Greeting VIPs at the beginning of your speech is customary.

   Humor is appreciated if it has subtle wit.

   Sensitive issues include religion and politics. Although Singaporeans will mention their strict fines for littering, chewing gum and not flushing the toilet, you had better not bring up these subjects. Instead, mention their accomplishments, including their top-ranking schools and superb airport but don't overdo it. During your speech your audience will be respectful.

   In your Question & Answer session, expect moderate participation with older audiences who were not used to raising hands at school. With younger people, participation will be livelier. Like many Asian cultures, Singaporeans will respond to your questions by trying to give you the answer you are seeking—there is a tendency towards harmony. You may not always elicit answers that are useful for you.

9. *Especially for women.* You will be well accepted in the business community, particularly if you are poised and speak in a composed voice.

10. *Comments.* Singaporeans are shrewd and rational in business and extremely well educated, better than many people they will be meeting from the West. Singaporeans have both British rooted and firm Asian traditions—creating an unusual mix of capabilities and qualities. They have strong organizational skills combined with the spiritual depth of most East and Southeast Asian people – which visitors tend to overlook as they pass shopping mall after shopping mall. Always reliable, Singaporeans appreciate frankness, honesty and modesty.

South Africa

1. In the business world, people are particular about *time*. Titles like "Director" aren't used in spoken communication, but "Doctor" and "Professor" are used.

2. First *names* are not always used upon meeting. Wait and see.

3. *Business cards* are exchanged when you meet but not in any set pattern.

4. In the business world, you greet by shaking hands.

5. *Business dress code* for men is dark suit or jacket and pants and dark shoes. White or light shirts and bright ties.

   Business dress code for women is suit or dress. Trouser suits are popular. Light but not overly bright colors.

6. To make a *toast*, say "cheers to the...," or in Afrikaans "*gesondheit*." If you receive a toast, say "thank you and cheers." If you are at a dinner party, you clink the glasses of those at your table. While you are at it, compliment them on their superb wines, both white and red of which they are justly proud.

7. *Non-verbal communication*. South Africans like people who have an informal and confident manner. Eye contact is direct.

8. *Your speech*. You might want to begin by saying, "Since I cannot address you in any or all of your 11 official languages, I shall restrict myself to English."

   Greeting VIPs at the beginning of your speech is customary.

   Humor is acceptable as long as you do not tread on sensitive issues.

   Sensitive issues include black empowerment, affirmative action, all religions, crime, the economy, rape and hijacking, Zimbabwe, foreign policy, emigration and international interference in local affairs.

   During your speech, do not be surprised if some people in the audience talk to each other or leave occasionally.

   In your Question & Answer session, you may have to encourage participation.

9. *Especially for women*: In South Africa, a fairly traditional attitude prevails. Enthusiasm is good, but not pushiness. South African culture is male-dominated.

10. *Comments*. A reference to South Africa as the "rainbow nation" would be appreciated as would recognition for South Africa's readiness to

integrate and adapt to change. Many South Africans are mad about sports, so praise for their athletic prowess and achievements would be well-accepted, especially a mention of their cricket, rugby and soccer teams. Trying to imitate the South African accent is not appreciated. Says Charlotte Stanton, "While most South Africans are striving to diminish the inequalities that still exist in South Africa, racial issues are not typically discussed in multi-racial settings. These discussions generally take place at home or among close friends."

South Korea

1. *Time* is sacred. Never be late when meeting a senior person.

2. First *names* are not used. In spoken communication *titles* such as Doctor, Professor, Ambassador, Chairman, Managing Director, Chief, Manager are used.

3. *Business cards* are exchanged even before sitting down. The senior person will initiate the exchange. With his right hand offering the card, he may touch your right arm as you reach for the card. This is a ceremonious event. Read the card when you receive it.

   Your business card should be English on one side and Korean on the other.

4. In the business world, Koreans *greet* by bowing. Sometimes two men will shake hands. A junior person will introduce you to a senior person you want to meet.

5. *Business dress code* for men is suit and tie.

   Dress code for women is business suit with long sleeves. Skirt below the knees. Stockings. Only wear short sleeves if it is a hot summer day.

6. To make a *toast*, say "I would like to make a toast to ABC Company and Chairman Kim for arranging this conference. I appreciate the opportunity to speak to you distinguished guests today."

To receive a toast, say, "Thank you, Chairman Lee for your kind toast. May I thank you for making this event possible. I appreciate your interest and hospitality."

In Korean 'cheers' is "*Kun Bae!*"

7. *Non-verbal communication.* Koreans like people who are respectful.

   Eye contact is indirect. Instead of looking in someone's eyes, you should look just under their eyes, at their cheeks. Avoid pointing and any broad gestures.

8. *Your speech.* As the speaker, you will be expected to sit with the most senior people. Be sure you are introduced properly and with due credit, otherwise your audience will not pay attention. Koreans are impressed by education, titles, and company names.

   To begin your talk, the general opening greeting in Korean is: "*Ahn nung ha shim ni ka.*" This works in any context, regardless of time, and is the most polite form.

   Instead of saying you are pleased to be in Korea, Yuri Lustenberger-Kim advises you to say "I thank you for honoring me with your attendance." Koreans focus on the act deserving attention so you should thank the audience for coming and thus allowing you to speak! "*Li jarirul chamsuk haeju shusuh dae danhi kamsahapnida.*"

   Greeting VIPs when you begin speaking is necessary.

   Sensitive issues include American troop presence in Korea (You can talk about the need for it, but any more detail——they do not care.), recent US stance with the North Korean regime, dense traffic, pollution, the Korean War, negative economic indicators.

   Audience reaction. During your speech, do not be surprised if your audience seems to sleep. Some close their eyes to listen more attentively.

   In your Question & Answer session, expect little participation because the older generation Koreans are not outspoken and do not want to "bother" you with questions. However, inquisitive and internationally-minded younger generation audience members will probably ask questions.

   You are expected to make a slight bow at the end of your speech.

9. *Especially for women*. If you are the speaker, you may be treated like a glass angel on a pedestal. Do not be offended if only women flock to you after your presentation; men do not know what to do. Other reminders: never be without stockings, no matter how hot it is. Wear lipstick in public and be sure your hair is neat looking.

10. *Comments*. Koreans will be pleased if you mention their cultural tradition of 5000 years or the enviable economic growth of the last two decades, Seoul as a leading Asian financial centre, or their recent successful co-hosting of the 2002 World Cup. Above all, be polite, respectful and natural.

Spain

1. Be on *time* but don't be offended if the other party arrives late. There are substantial differences between the North and South of Spain. In the North time schedules are more respected. Barcelona is considered a business city without as much socializing as in Madrid.

2. First *names* can be used upon meeting but respect must be shown in tone of voice. Also, *"Ustes"*, the polite form of "you" must be used. Spaniards have two surnames, their father's first surname followed by their mother's first surname. In the example Antonio Franco Alonso, Franco is Antonio's father's name and Alonso is his mother's name. In business, he might use only 'Señor Franco.' For a woman named Maria Fernandez Pol, Fernandez is her father's name and Pol her mother's name. If she marries Antonio, she keeps both names and may add 'de Franco.' In business, she will continue to use 'Señora Fernandez.' In spoken communication, a medical doctor is "Doctor" but the accent should be on "tor". Senior, highly respected and typically elder individuals may use *"Don"* as in "Don Rodrigues".

3. *Business cards* are exchanged when you meet.

4. In the business world, you shake hands.

5. *Business dress code* for men is a conservative and elegant suit. Dark colors are preferred.

Business dress code for women is a dark or soft colored suit with elegant blouse and scarf. Skirt not above the knees. Neither too much jewelry nor make-up. The more conservative the better.

Spanish are fashion conscious. Your clothes will be noticed.

6. To make a *toast*, you raise your glass and say *"Salud"* (health), *"Enhorabuena,"* (congratulations), or *"Por muchos años"* (for many years to come) and clink glasses. Make eye contact.

   If you receive a toast, raise your glass and respond *"Gracias"* (thank you). A few words in return are appreciated.

7. *Non-verbal communication.* Spanish like people who are respectful and protocol oriented.

8. *Your speech.* To begin in Spanish say, *"Buenos dias/buenas tardes, señoras y señores."* ("Good morning/afternoon ladies and gentlemen.")

   "Es para mi un placer estar aqui, en ..." (name of place) or *"Estoy encantado de estar aqui, en ..."* (It is a pleasure to be here in ...)

   "Es un verdadero placer el estar con Uds." ("It is a pleasure to be here.")

   Greeting VIPs at the beginning of your speech is customary.

   Humor can be used in the business world but it must be polite and not related to cultural or gender issues.

   Sensitive issues include politics and religion.

   In your Question & Answer session, expect little participation.

9. *Especially for women.* As a business woman in Spain, you will be treated with respect. You can accept courtesy and compliments from men. You may also be kissed on the hand by men.

10. *Comments.* What you can do to really impress is to be knowledgeable of the cultural differences between regions. Spain is very rich in tradition, art and history. Food and wine are part of the culture. Spending time after meals is very appreciated if you know how to enjoy that time. If you are interested in sports, soccer can be a good ice-breaker. Be aware of the deep rivalry between Madrid and Barcelona. In Madrid, Castilian Spanish is spoken. In Barcelona,

Catalan is the language. It was formerly considered a dialect but now is used even at university. Do not use *"vos"* in Spanish which is a literary term that is rarely used anymore.

Sweden

1. *Time* is respected.

2. First *names* are usually used upon meeting, but if you come from a country where surnames are used, Swedish people may adapt to your custom. In spoken communication, *titles* are not used.

3. *Business cards* are exchanged when you meet.

4. In the business world, you *greet* by shaking hands.

5. *Business dress code* for men is suit or jacket with tie. *Business dress code* for women is a suit or trouser suit with long sleeves. In upper management, women wear stockings.

   Generally speaking, Swedish people dress informally, but they do have formal dinners where men wear tails and women wear long evening dresses. If your agenda includes such an event, ascertain what the proper dress code is. At formal dinners, your country's traditional costume can substitute for formal wear.

6. To make a *toast* say *"Skoal."* If you receive a toast, say *"Tack"* and give a small speech. Never toast your host or anyone senior to you in rank or age until they toast you, nor must you touch your drink until the host has said *"skoal."* When a toast is made at a dinner party, the woman first looks to her left, and the man looks to his right so "pairs" toast each other. In days gone-by, when a communal mug was passed around, each person calculated how much they could drink while leaving enough so that everyone at the table had their fair share. This attitude of consensus prevails today (even though you get your own glass!)

7. *Non-verbal communication.* Swedes like people who are open-minded. Eye contact is direct. Swedes feel more comfortable with some distance between them and you.

8. *Your speech.* To begin in Swedish: "*God Morgon/God Dag, mina damer och herrar*" (Good morning/afternoon, ladies and gentlemen). "*Det är en ära att få vara här*" (It is a pleasure to be here).

Greeting VIPs is not customary.

Swedish humor tends to be sophisticated and dry in the John Cleese British style (rather than American or German style).

None of the respondents could think of any issue which cannot be discussed openly.

In your Question & Answer session, expect moderate participation. Swedish people tend to hold back.

9. *Especially for women.* If you asked a Swedish woman if she felt equal to her male counterpart, the very question would surprise her. It would surprise a man, too. Men and women are considered equal. They are raised that way and treat each other that way.

10. *Comments.* When you are speaking, be open, direct and lively. At first you may get a subdued response, but if you continue with energy, Swedish people will open up and appreciate the effort you have made for them. They may appear slow in conversation; do not be deluded. They are using the time to think through the implications of what you are saying.

Switzerland

1. *Time* is sacred. Be punctual or, even better, two minutes early. The Swiss, though punctual, tend to be slow, but methodical.

2. Most Swiss business people would prefer not to use first *names* upon meeting, but they are used to accommodating other customs. They will commit your first and surname to memory so remember their name, too. *Titles* are not normally used in spoken communication.

3. There is no set time to exchange *business cards.*

4. In the business world, you *greet* by shaking hands.

5. *Business dress code* for men is a dark or light-colored suit and tie. (In banking, it is still dark suits.) *Business dress code* for

women is a business suit with skirt or trousers. Stockings are usually worn. In the "back office," however, dress code is very relaxed with trendy outfits, jeans and teeshirts.

6. Making *toasts* is important. To make a toast, raise your glass and give a small speech. At the end of your toast, say "*Zum Wohl*" (in German), "*Santé*" in French and "*Salute*" in Italian. It is customary to "clink" glasses with everyone at your table before drinking. You must look people in the eye. To reply, thank your host for the kind words.

7. *Non-verbal communication.* Swiss like people who have a rather formal manner at first meeting. Eye contact is direct. Avoid touching people unless you know them very well.

8. *Your speech.* In the Swiss German-speaking part, begin with "*Grüezi mitenand*" which means "Hello everybody." In the French-speaking part, say "*Bonjour, mesdames et messieurs*." In the Ticino, which is Italian-speaking, begin with "*buon giorno.*"

Greeting VIPs is customary.

Swiss humor tends to be very broad, but as a foreigner you must tread gently. Avoid jokes about Switzerland or other nationalities (20 percent of the population are foreigners, and xenophobia exists).

Sensitive issues include their position as an "island of neutrality," high prices, money laundering, bank secrecy, and dealings with Germany in WWI.

During your speech, do not be surprised if your audience is unresponsive. The Swiss are reserved and subdued but very well-intentioned people. If you persevere, you may win them over.

9. *Especially for women.* Women are treated with respect but find it difficult to achieve senior positions. Some men still feel that women should stick to the 3 Ks (in English, "children, the kitchen and the church"), and should not work if they have children. Elisabeth Marksteiner says, "You are unlikely to experience overt discrimination, but I was disconcerted when a Swiss businessman told me that women should not have received the vote in 1971 because we are over-emotional."

10. *Comments.* The biggest natural resource of Switzerland is its people. The society is well-ordered and highly structured, even more so than in Germany. In business dealings Swiss are methodical and strive for perfection. They may be negative, even defensive when confronted with a new proposal: "We have never done it that way, we have always done it this way. If we agree, who knows what will happen next!" Try to understand the immense cultural diversity in this small land. Avoid calling French-speaking Swiss "French." They are "Suisses Romands." Strong rivalry exists between the Swiss German and the Suisses Romands, with the latter often more open-minded.

Avoid incorrect clichés: the Swiss are tired of jokes about Lederhosen (which are Bavarian, not Swiss), and the cuckoo clock is from the Black Forest in Southern Germany, contrary to what Harry Lime said in "The Third Man." To impress, mention a Swiss personality like Henri Dunant (founder of the Red Cross) or CG Jung (founder of a school of psychoanalysis) or their 2003 victory in the America's Cup—somewhat incongruous for a landlocked country!

Thailand

1. *Time* is flexible.

2. First *names* may be used upon meeting but do not initiate it. When you use the first name, it is polite to put "khun" before the first name (Khun Michael or Khun Sarah). Titles are often used in spoken communication. Some people like to be addressed as "Doctor," especially those who received the title without going to school.

3. *Business cards* are exchanged upon meeting, with a slight bow.

4. With Westerners, Thais are quite comfortable shaking hands; however, they traditionally greet by pressing their hands together and bowing slightly. As you bow, if you are a man, say, "*Sawasdee Khrap.*" If you are a woman, say, "*Sawasdee Ka.*" To make any phrase more polite, Thais end with these gender-specific terms of respect. (It makes no difference which gender you are addressing.) So again, "Khrap" is what a man says and "Ka" is what a woman speaker says.

5. *Business dress code* for men is suit and tie. *Business dress code* for women is suit, long sleeves, knee-length skirt, preferably

in Thai silk. An interesting fact is that yellow is the color of royalty, since both the current king and the former king were born on Monday. (Each day of the week has a special color: Monday: yellow, Tuesday: pink, Wednesday: green, Thursday: orange, Friday: light blue, Saturday: violet, and Sunday: red.)

6. To make a *toast*, say *"Khorb Khun Khrap"* if you are a man. A woman says, *"Khorb Khun Kha"* (adding the feminine term of respect). Or you can say *"Chai yo"* which is "Cheers!" To reply, say "thank you" and toast back.

7. *Non-verbal communication.* Thais like people who have a respectful manner. Avoid speaking loudly. Eye contact is indirect. Avoid patting children on the head. The head is sacred and demands respect. Do not walk over things that are lying on the floor like a book or hand-bag. Avoid pointing a finger, crossing your legs or using your foot to point out something. Feet are considered profane. Avoid having the sole of your shoe visible to other people or even to a picture of the Royal family or the Thai flag which is perceived as a major insult.

8. *Your speech.* Greeting words in Thai: A woman says, *"Sawasdee Ka."* A man says, *"Sawasdee Khrap."*

   Greeting VIPs is customary.

   Humor is appreciated if it is witty and gentle. Avoid jokes about the Royal Family and monarchy, racism and sexism.

   Sensitive issues are politics and prostitution.

   During your speech, do not be surprised if some in your audience talk to each other.

   In Question & Answer sessions, expect limited participation.

9. *Especially for women.* In the business context, women and men are treated equally. Socially, the Thai way usually prevails. As a woman keep a low profile, be polite and feminine

10. *Comments.* It is a very serious offence to ridicule the Royal family. Do not criticize or make jokes about them. Heed a Thai expression to "Keep a cool heart. Be patient."— *"chai yen chailon."* Thais are highly relationship-oriented and prefer to conduct business with people with whom they are comfortable, even if it comes at the expense of slight losses. Hard negotiation tactics are frowned upon.

Turkey

1. In Turkey, *time* is flexible, especially in Istanbul where you can be stuck in traffic.

2. First *names* are used in the business world followed by a gender-specific word of respect. For example, John Smith would be "John bey." Rita Green would be "Rita hanim." In official situations like state dinners, "Sayin" with title followed by the last name is used ("Sayin Bakan Smith" for a government minister).

3. There is no set time to exchange *business cards*.

4. In the business world, you greet by firmly shaking hands.

5. Proper *dress code* is normal Western European standard: For men, shirt, suit, and tie. For women, modest business suit and heels. No short skirts.

6. *Toasts* vary to a great degree in Turkey, depending on the circumstances. Follow the lead of your hosts. Common toasts include *"Sherefe"*, which means "to your honor" and *"Sagliginiza"* which means "to your health." Looking at the way the men toast their glasses might be important. If you want to be humble you would hold your glass a little lower than the other person's glass at the moment of toasting.

7. *Non-verbal communication.* Turkish people make lots of movements while talking and there are only a few gestures to avoid. Putting your thumb between your second and third finger is offensive. Making your left hand into a fist and hitting it with your right hand (like getting ketchup by hitting the bottom of the bottle) is very offensive. A man touching another man is accepted, but a woman touching a man is considered flirting. A woman staring at a man is considered provocative. A man who stares at a woman might upset her male companion.

8. *Your speech.* A standard start would be *"Sayin dinleyiciler"* (Dear audience) or *"Sayin misafirler"* (Dear guests). A friendlier start would be *"Sevgili katilimcilar"* (Dear attendees) or *"Herkese Merhaba"* (Hello to everyone). To continue in the friendly manner say, *"Burada sizlerle birlikte olmaktan cok mutluyum"* (I am very happy to be together with you here).

VIPs should be greeted at the beginning of your speech.

Humor related to the subject is appreciated.

Sensitive issues include Greek, Armenian, Kurdish relations and human rights.

During your speech, audience reaction may vary. Turks are very attentive listeners. Expect applause or even cheers at the end. If they lose interest, they will talk to each other.

9. *Especially for women.* Turkish businessmen and businesswomen are equal. Turkish women are not afraid to speak their minds but they still are respectful. If a woman looks directly in the eyes of a man whom she doesn't know, for example, passing on the street, it is considered flirting and might easily be understood as "come and talk to me." To avoid this, don't stare at men. Off-color jokes are in bad taste for women to tell.

10. *Comments.* Turkey is poised between two worlds, just as Istanbul spans two continents. This juxtaposition between modern and traditional is felt in industry as well as culturally and intellectually. The Asian part is called "Anatolia" which means "full of mothers." Turkey has been the cradle of numerous civilizations. The oldest known human settlement is in Catalhoyuk (7500BC). Turks introduced coffee to Europe and tulips to Holland. Legend has it that Noah's Ark landed in Eastern Turkey. Homer and Aesop were born in Turkey. Forward-thinking Turks are proud of their rich civilization and are trying to change the image of Turkey from the "sick men of Europe" during the Ottoman Empire's declining years to a youthful, western, vibrant republic.

The United Arab Emirates

1. *Time* is very flexible. As a speaker, be ready to begin on time but do not be surprised at considerable delays.

2. To address someone, use their last *name* preceded by Mr. or Mrs. Example: Mr. Al-Mulla. *Titles* such as Doctor and Sheikh are used. Doctor plus surname: Doctor Al-Mulla. Sheikh plus given name: Sheikh Mohammed. (Sheikh was originally the head of a clan but in the business world is used by anyone of importance.)

3. *Business cards* are exchanged upon meeting.

4. In the business world, you *greet* by shaking hands.

5. *Business dress code* for men is suit with tie. *Business dress code* for women is a conservative suit with long sleeves and skirt below the knees.

6. Alcohol is not consumed so *toasts* do not officially exist. At a private event, if your host *toasts* you by saying, "*Sahha*," the correct reply is, "*Sahhatane.*"

7. *Non-verbal communication.* Eye contact is direct. Pointing is very rude. Sitting so that the soles of your shoes are exposed is a great insult.

8. *Your speech.* Although Arabic is the official language, 70 percent of the population are foreigners, so English is the "glue" that connects the various groups.

   Greeting VIPs at the beginning of your speech is mandatory.

   Speech-making is an extremely serious business. Humor is not acceptable.

   Sensitive issues include the need for more democracy and criticizing the ruler or his family.

9. *Especially for women.* You will be accepted as a professional business woman but do not expect to establish friendships. Even if you are offered alcohol at a private event, it is better not to accept.

10. *Comments.* The United Arab Emirates consist of seven sheikhdoms: Abu Dhabi, Ajman, Dubai, Fujaira, Ras al-Khaimah, Sharjah and Umm al-Qaiwain. The atmosphere in the UAE is very cosmopolitan. Many Arabs are highly educated and hold degrees from American or British universities. They expect you to deliver an intelligent and thoughtful message. Avoid lecturing or speaking in a condescending manner, which is considered arrogant. It is impolite to ask about an Arab's wife or family unless you know them.

United States of America

1. In the business world, *time* is money. Americans want everything fast, especially results. Although they may appear
   relaxed and informal, the clock is running. In cities "24/7"
   prevails which means shops and services are available around the
   clock, seven days a week. Even then it's not possible to accomplish
   everything.

2. First *names* are used upon meeting. Americans may shorten or
   "Americanize" your name without asking. ("Elizabeth" becomes
   "Liz" and "Gerhard" becomes "Gary") If you prefer your complete
   name, say so. Americans aren't as good at remembering surnames as
   Europeans are. In spoken communication, academic and medical as
   well as elected and appointed government officials' titles are used .

3. In the United States, *business cards* are usually exchanged.

4. In the business world, men and women greet by shaking hands
   firmly.

5. *Business dress code* for men is suit and tie. The financial and
   legal world has a more conservative dress code again since
   the DotComs tumbled. Many firms have have casual Fridays
   (khakis with collared shirt, no shorts, etc.) In these situations, men
   keep a jacket and tie in their office in case they have an unscheduled
   visitor who requires formality. Conferences at resort hotels may
   request "business casual," which needs clarification. It may mean
   jackets without ties or polo shirts and chinos. American men do not
   wear the "expensive blazer and jeans" combination seen in Europe.
   Business dress code for women is suit, coordinates or pants suit. More
   black and navy blue on the East Coast and in finance and law firms.
   More color elsewhere. Air conditioning works at maximum strength
   in conference rooms, so a long-sleeved jacket or a wrap is useful.

6. Except at formal dinners, Americans usually do not *toast*.
   They will rarely raise a glass or look you in the eye as is customary in many other countries.

7. *Non-verbal communication*. Americans like people who have an outgoing and direct manner. Eye contact is direct.

8. *Your speech*. Greeting VIPs at the beginning of your speech is customary. Know who the dignitaries are, especially elected officials and address them with title.

    Americans enjoy humor in presentations. They like to listen to can-do messages and personal success stories.

    Sensitive issues include abortion, obesity, smoking, gun laws, religion, foreign policy and minorities.

    In your Question & Answer session, expect lively participation. A British respondent said, "If you ask Americans to stand on their chairs, they will comply."

    To really impress, be knowledgeable about baseball, professional football and sports in general!

9. *Especially for women*. You may be surprised by the seriousness of business women who are striving for equality with men. Light-hearted conversation ("flirting") between men and women is scarce.

10. *Comments*. Many Americans are poor listeners. They have short attention spans and rely on sound bites. You may need to repeat what you are saying. Be aware of "political correctness." Be wary of making comments which have sexual innuendoes. Women prefer to be called "women" not "ladies." Americans often neglect to respond (RSVP) to invitations even when they plan to come. It is common to follow up any formal invitation by phone. As friendly as most Americans are, do not be offended if someone says "let's have lunch" and never calls.

Conclusion

Speaking to an audience is a unique opportunity to influence people, to change minds, to touch a chord. After all, when a global crisis strikes, does the prime minister send a fax? No, he makes a statement to the press. When we announce new scientific breakthroughs, do we send an E-mail? No, we present a paper in front of an audience. When we recognize someone's outstanding achievements, do we call her? No, we organize an awards ceremony and honor the recipient with a speech. In fact, the laureate is usually expected to make a speech, too.

This book tells you what it takes to prepare, practice and present a compelling speech. However, like a scuba-diving manual or a cook book, *Speaking Globally* does you little good sitting on a shelf. The material needs to be put to work.

So accept the challenge! And start speaking for yourself. The ability to communicate well at the lectern is a highly sought-after commodity. Good speakers are in great demand. As soon as the word gets around that you can capture the minds of your listeners and inspire them with your subject, you will go places both in your career and around the globe.

When you do put the guidelines in *Speaking Globally* into practice, you will connect with your audience. You will know you have succeeded because you will hear the words:

Irie Speech!

ありがとうございます

Congratulazioni!

تهانينا

Mahusay!

Goed gesproken!

Vel gjort!

Bravo!

축하합니다

Kitünö

Bakus sekali!

Parabens!

Congratulations!

祝贺

Countdown for Your Speaking Assignment

Six Weeks in Advance

Get the necessary details:

- When and where are you speaking?
- What is the subject of your speech?
- What is your time slot and time limit?
- Who else is on the program?
- Who is your audience?

Determine your desired end results:

- What do want your audience to do when you finish speaking?
- How do you want to come across?
- What do you want your audience to remember two weeks later?

Analyze your audience and determine their WIIFM.

Four Weeks in Advance

Create your speech:

- Choose a format.
- Collect and deal with the data.

❧ Decide how to begin your speech.

❧ Position yourself differently from the other speakers.

❧ Personalize your message with a story and/or humor.

❧ Create a powerful ending. Put the most important word last.

Choose your visual aids.

Start getting your voice and body in shape:

❧ Practice the 3-B exercises to control nerves.

❧ If you want to lower the pitch of your voice, start now!

Send off the Speaker's Checklist for Success.

Practice Session No. 1:

❧ Practice your speech out loud and time it.

❧ Review and make changes.

❧ Write speaker notes.

Two Weeks in Advance

Write "suggested" introductory remarks and send to person who will introduce you.

Business cards and handout materials should be ready.

Practice Session No. 2:

❧ Rehearse your speech out loud. If you are like many of my clients, you will resist doing this. Performance can best be improved by performing, not by reading your speaker notes silently at your desk or in the transit lounge. If possible, videotape yourself. When you watch yourself afterwards, remember that the video camera is objective: it records what it sees. If you need to work on your delivery style, begin now.

❧ Condense your speaker notes.

If required, send your manuscript, as well as special terms and words for interpreters.

Confirm travel plans: Passport, visas, ticket, money.

One Week in Advance

Your slides should be ready. Do not change them. (Visual aids do not make the difference between an acceptable speech and a memorable one. You do.) Select what you will wear. If necessary, get a hair cut (hair needs time to "settle in").

Practice Session No. 3:
Have you practiced your speech yet? You need to practice it out loud in a large room. You need to practice with the visual aids you will be using on the day. Why not ask your secretary and your department to sit in? I know you will resist. It never fails to amaze me how many speakers try to avoid practice sessions. Would you enter a marathon without even running round the block? Would you climb the Matterhorn without breaking in new hiking boots? Shall I continue? Please practice your speech. From start to finish. Out loud. Now.

Three Days in Advance

Practice Session No. 4:
"Over the top" rehearsal. Deliver your speech with great urgency and use expansive gestures. In short, exaggerate. If you videotape yourself, you may discover that only now you have attained the "energy level" necessary to reach a large audience.

The Day Before

If your presentation is in a distant city, you should arrive now.

- ☙ Check out the conference room and equipment.
- ☙ The best way to ensure tomorrow's success is to run through your speech with visual aids and microphone in the actual conference room.
- ☙ If you will begin in the local language, get help with pronunciation.
- ☙ If you will name VIPs, be sure your information is accurate.
- ☙ Get a good night's sleep.

On the Big Day

Double-check your slides, notes, handouts, reading glasses.
Be sure you can answer "Yes" to the following questions:

● Are the chairs positioned so that everyone can see you?

● Do you know how to use the equipment?

● Can you adjust the microphone?

● Is there enough light where you will be standing?

● Can you be seen if you walk around?

● Are there any potential distractions?

● Do you know where the telephone and the toilets are?

● Have you asked catering to stop serving while you are speaking?

Introduce yourself to the interpreters and ask if they have any questions.
Before you speak, mingle with your audience and introduce yourself.

Giving Your Speech

Stride...

● Deliver your message with power and comfort.

● Handle difficult situations with ease.

● Keep your Question & Answer session lively and pertinent.

and Glide!

Afterwards

Don't leave immediately. Stay for networking opportunities.
Write thank you notes.

Evaluate your speech:

● Did your audience react the way you wanted them to?

● Did you come across the way you wanted to?

● Two weeks later, ask some attendees what they remember from your talk. Their answers may be enlightening.

II

Last-Minute Changes

If you are reading this in flight on the way to a conference where you are speaking, you still have time to improve a speech you are about to deliver. Using these step-by-step, practical and proven techniques, you can make subtle changes and achieve noteworthy success at the lectern.

Warm Up for Take Off ...

1. First, forgive yourself in advance for any mistakes you might make. Public speaking is a live performance. Nobody expects you to be perfect. Your audience wants you to be interesting, informative and in control. If you give the impression that you are comfortable, they will relax. Then you will begin to relax, and it will be much easier to get your message across.

2. Carefully note how the speaker preceding you attaches the microphone or switches on the overhead projector. You want to be competent when it is your turn to take the stage.

3. Don't underestimate the benefit of doing some controlled breathing. You can do this exercise quite inconspicuously while you are waiting to be introduced. Start by gently pushing the used-up oxygen out of your lungs. Then inhale slowly and carefully. When your lungs are filled with fresh air, hold for a count of three (or you might hyperventilate). Repeat this exercise three times. These deep breaths will slow down your racing heartbeat and increase the supply of oxygen to your brain.

4. Let there be light! Is there enough light on the area where you will be standing? In all probability, the room is half-dark to accommodate slides. If you can locate a technician (usually sitting at the back of the room or in a booth), ask him to turn up the lights when you begin. This accomplishes three things. The audience can see you. You can see the audience. You demonstrate you are in control of your surroundings.

Taking Off ...

1. As you are introduced, stride to the front of the room with energy and authority. Put your script on the lectern. Then plant both feet firmly on the ground. Get a look on your face that says, "I am delighted to be here, and I have a great message for you."

2. Wait until all eyes are on you before you open your mouth. This is the most important thing you can do to establish your credibility. Audiences have short attention spans and even worse memories. You want them paying attention when you start. If you have the courage to do this, it will have a powerful effect on you and your audience. All you do is wait until the room goes very quiet. Then begin speaking. This is so important that I am going to repeat it: wait until all eyes are on you before you open your mouth.

3. So far, so good. Here's another challenge. With the very first words you say, give yourself permission to gesture. With both hands. Let your random energy become positive and focused. You will probably ignore this suggestion. But if you do try it, you will wonder why you didn't get your pent-up energy flowing years ago.

4. Your introductory remarks are important. If you are in a culture where greeting honored guests is expected, do so. Respecting customs is important. If you haven't prepared an attention-grabbing introduction, at least deliver your first words with vigor and verve (and gesture with both hands).

At this late stage, resist making major changes to your presentation.

In Flight ...

As you speak, incorporate these suggestions. Your audience will be grateful.

1. Speak with energy. Enthusiasm is contagious. It's hard for an audience to tune you out when you exude interest in your own speech.

2. Incorporate pauses:

   ❀ When you pause beforehand, you signal that something notewor-thy is coming.

   ❀ When you pause afterwards, you give your audience a chance to let your words sink in.

   ❀ When you pause, you are in control. It's like strolling through a park. If you are nervous, you will rush through and not take time to smell the roses.

   ❀ Pauses = power. It's that simple.

3. Include verbal signposts to keep you and your audience on track:

   ❀ "Having reviewed last quarter's figures, let's move on to the cur-rent situation."

   ❀ "Here's the second reason for my decision."

   ❀ "Let's take a look at the final option."

4. Highlight important concepts with your voice and your well-chosen words:

   ❀ Let me *underline*...''

   ❀ "My *take-home message* is..."

   ❀ "If you *remember one thing* from my speech..."

5. Look at your audience. In a two-way conversation, someone can ask you to explain what you mean. Audiences cannot do that, so you have to listen to them with your eyes. Especially in multilingual, culturally-diverse situations, you have to keep a constant check. Are they con-fused? Bored? Furious? You may need to repeat a phrase, speed up or slow down.

6. One last suggestion. How about a little smile? At least a pleasant look on your face.

A Smooth Landing ...

1. Give the audience some advance notice before you finish by saying, "In conclusion," or "Before I end..."

2. Leave your audience with a strong statement or provocative question. This is your final chance to make a lasting impression. (Add "thank you" after your last words, but don't substitute "thank you" for a dynamic ending.)

Index

Aha! So you read the end first?! It is a fast way to get a feel for the book so you can decide whether to buy it.

Unfortunately your audience cannot do the same when you speak. They have to listen to you from start to finish.

You need to get their attention instantly and keep them enthralled until your very last word. *Speaking Globally* will help you do just that!

For information about Speaking Unlimited programs and keynote addresses, please contact:

Speaking Unlimited
312.913.9071
beth@speakingunlimited.com
www.speakingunlimited.com